PURSUING TIMELESS AGILITY

The Path to Lasting Agile Transformation

JIMMIE BUTLER

Pursuing Timeless Agility:
The Path to Lasting Agile Transformation

Acknowledgments

First and foremost, I thank God, my Lord and Savior Jesus Christ, for blessing me with the ability and the opportunity to take on this project. He helped me recognize when there were more important things to do than write, and gave me perspective that reduced the stress from my own pressure to finish ahead of all else.

I thank my wife Amanda for being so supportive of the time and effort I spent writing this book. She is a gift from God and a wonderful life partner.

Thanks also to:

Melissa Northern for providing editorial review and support.

CONTENTS

Introduction

Agile transformation is hard to achieve. Amen? It is especially difficult when the common notion of what that means is misconstrued. When someone says they are Agile, we can no longer take for granted that we know what they mean. Ask ten different people to define Agile and Agile transformation, and you will get at least a few different answers. Many organizations believe that Agile is the answer to *something*, yet many are misaligned with the true meaning and intent of Agile. Once upon a time, the struggle was to get Agile in the door. Today, the struggle is to correct the unbridled distortion of Agile and to help undo the damage that misunderstanding has inflicted.

Teams have flocked to Agile to do software development better, but are they really delivering better products? Is your organization always working on the next right thing? Are your teams learning how to deliver the *right things* more effectively and efficiently? There are many ways to achieve the goal of delivering the right things, and then to deliver them more frequently, yet few achieve it. Some become better at the more frequently part, but fall short on doing the *right* things. Others continue to struggle in all facets of product development. The "Certification Economy" is partly to blame. In order to get the proverbial *Agile foot in the door*, early compromises were made to make Agile more palatable for traditional organizations. These compromises have become the norm – despite the divergence from the true intent of Agile.

Organizations love to buy neatly packaged *"solutions"* that promise to fix their problems. Many believe that merely implementing standardized tools and practices will bring a whole new level of success. Frameworks and certifications around structured methodologies come and go and have been changing as long as I can remember. The *"silver bullet"* keeps changing.

The more I think about that previous statement, the more convinced I am that it sums up the perpetual problems we face in our organizations. I have come to believe that organizational obsession with buzzwords, frameworks, and certifications are ultimately the reason why organizations fail to achieve true organizational agility in whatever they do. *Agile* is just one of the more recent topics that touches all three.

Rampant distortion and misuse of Agile has led some coaches to say that Agile is dead. It is not so much that they no longer believe in what Agile represents. Listen to the values and methods these coaches embrace and what you hear *will be* Agile. Rather, they believe that the *word* "Agile" is so abused, misunderstood, and misapplied that the term is no longer effective – confusing. It is true, what many call Agile today is not Agile. I do not believe running away from the term is the solution. The values and principles of the Agile Manifesto[1] are timeless – when would you ever *not* prefer what the Manifesto recommends? When would an empirical approach ever *not* be the best way to iterate on and produce the *right* things? Maybe you cannot answer those questions just yet. That is ok. I will expound upon these in the first chapter when I explain what Agile *really* is, and why it is timeless.

What you will learn in this book is that Agile is NOT dead. What you think Agile is, however, may be challenged or expanded. If I do my job well, you will approach concepts you think you understand from a different perspective. The way I think may not be *right* or *best,* but hopefully it helps you to get *better* in your quest for Agile transformation.

I believe that *Mindset Transcends Methodology™*. Your understanding impacts what you do and how you do it. What you believe and value is the foundation from which all else derives. How you do your work will change over time as you learn and grow, but *why* you do what you do transcends all of those changes. Until your organization collectively bases everything it does off of that foundational mindset, it will never achieve true organizational agility, or Timeless Agility.

Timeless Agility is the outcome of a mindset that transcends methodology. It consistently allows you to effectively and efficiently identify, produce, and deliver the next right thing.

To attain Timeless Agility, that elusive organizational agility, your entire organization needs to think differently. Agile transformation, therefore, is going to be more about transforming minds than practices. Some will say adopting new practices leads to new mindsets. That can certainly happen in parallel within development teams. However, non-development teams do not follow the same practices. Organizational agility requires everyone working from the same mindset. I will dig deeper into being enterprise-aware in Chapter Three, What is Timeless Agility?

The first half of this book focuses on what Agile *really* is, what much of industry thinks it is and how they *do* it, and then aims to help you see where your current thinking and activity fits within all of that. I believe you must first recognize what problem you need to solve before you take steps in a different direction. As I hope you will see in Chapters Four and Five, the "do then become" Agile argument is not always a sound approach. What many organizations are doing does not align with what Agile intended in the first place. Teams cannot *become* Agile if what they are doing is *not* Agile.

The latter half of the book provides practical advice for how to move your organization toward Timeless Agility. Pursuing Timeless Agility is about establishing the foundations that will stand the test of time, outlive the latest *"best practices,"* and allow you to roll from one paradigm shift to another without losing your organizational agility. I will provide some insight on how to begin, and how to progress. The guidance includes both approach and tactics. Lastly, the final, and largest, chapter focuses on how to measure success. What I suggest goes against the grain of *"common wisdom."* Like anything else in this book, consume it with an open mind and evaluate it accordingly.

A slight shift in perspective changes everything.

I assume you desire organizational agility and transformation, but there are obstacles keeping you from realizing that vision. Rest assured, you are not alone. Very few organizations have actually achieved organization-wide transformation. I think many are on the wrong path altogether. Certifications are not a guarantee of success. Despite the Project Management Professional (PMP) ® certification having been around since 1984, many organizations still fail to perform traditional project management really well. The path to Agile transformation is no different. I tell you this, not to diminish your hope, but to highlight the fact that transformation is challenging. Perhaps the common approaches and thought processes taught are not necessarily what you should emulate. To get over that proverbial hump, it is time to look at this from a different perspective. This book will show you Agile through a different lens than you may be wearing right now. Embrace it and evaluate for yourself.

Before You Begin

❖ Write down the problem you are trying to solve by reading this book. We will refer back to this later.

❖ Find three to five other people to read this book with to strategically tag-team on transformation. A team pushing change is stronger than you alone.

❖ Keep an open mind. Never say, "that will not work here." Consider how every idea could be applied.

I encourage you to think very carefully about what problem you are trying to solve by reading this book. Put some solid thought into it and write it down somewhere that you can reference back to later. There are two primary reasons I am asking you to write this down. For starters, I am a firm believer that before you spend any time, effort, and money on something, you should have an understanding of what problem you are trying to solve, or what opportunity you are trying to capture with that effort. Secondly, one of the goals of this book, and something I do as a coach, is to challenge whether or not you are focused on the *right* problem, or opportunity. If you are not focused on the right thing, for the right reason, what you *do* cannot achieve your desired outcome. Please feel free to put the book down right now and capture that problem statement for yourself. Later in the book, I will ask you to revisit that problem statement to see if you would write it differently.

Section One:
Understanding the Problem

"If you are unable to understand the cause of a problem, it is impossible to solve it."

-Naoto Kan

Chapter 1:
What is Agile...Really?

The word "Agile" is mentioned over 700 times between the covers of this book, so defining what Agile *really is* seems like the right place to start. The data, as well as my experience, suggests that despite already *"doing Agile"*, many organizations do not understand what Agile really is. This common misunderstanding leads to misapplication, and organizations struggle as a result.

Within coaching circles, there are plenty of concepts and practices to debate ad nauseam. I believe none of them are more polarizing, and important, than the meaning and proper practice of Agile. Competent coaches do not argue as much over the meaning of Agile as they do the fact that the true meaning and intent has been hijacked and misused by what I call the "Certification Economy." I will explore this *"common wisdom"* and its effects in the following chapters. For now, let us explore what Agile *really is* and intends to accomplish.

"To me, 'Agile' isn't a set of practices. It's what we described in the Manifesto, using Values and Principles. It's a way of thinking, a spirit or manner of behaving."[2]
– Ron Jeffries, co-author, Agile Manifesto

Agile = The Agile Manifesto

In February of 2001, seventeen people from different organizations convened with one thing in common – they all were actively working in ways that provided an alternative to traditional documentation-driven software development. Their *how* was different, but their *why* was essentially the same. These collective values and principles needed a name, thus "Agile" was born. Their discussion and the resulting agreement on the values and principles they embodied officially became the "Manifesto for Agile Software Development", otherwise known simply as the "Agile Manifesto" or "Manifesto."

   "Agile" is often used as a noun, a verb, an adjective, an idea, a methodology, and a mindset. You may have heard terms such as, the Agile methodology, Agile development team, Agile project management, Agile Business Analyst, Agile Coach, Agile Scrum, Agile mindset, Agile system, doing Agile, and being Agile. It seems the word "Agile" is used to describe just about everything, but is that appropriate?

"Let's use 'Agile' to mean
'consistent with the Manifesto.'" [3]
– Ron Jeffries, co-author, Agile Manifesto

   Agile originated as a set of four value statements and twelve corresponding principles that shared a common purpose across several pre-existing methodologies, yet Agile itself is methodology *independent*. The Agile Manifesto does not include or suggest processes, practices, or tools for how to best live out those principles – to do so would not be Agile. What you *do* day-to-day can align with Agile and it can also not align with Agile – your framework does not make you Agile.

Many Agile concepts and practices pre-date the Agile Manifesto – the Manifesto merely coalesced these values and principles into the mainstream. Some will argue the Manifesto is limiting and beyond its time. Others, like me, suggest it remains a vital part of one's foundation. These values and principles seem timeless to me, as I cannot imagine a time when I would not prefer what the Manifesto recommends.

Ron Jeffries, co-author of the Agile Manifesto, states that Agile *is* the Manifesto, the values and principles defined therein, but also acknowledges that the Manifesto is *"not the whole of 'Agile'"* – that Agile grows. In Ron's opinion, *"people are devising new values, principles, ideas and tools all the time. These may well be consistent with the Manifesto. When they are, we call them 'Agile.'"* Notice the key here – only when things are consistent with the Manifesto may they be considered "Agile."

I believe the Manifesto is something to embrace as part of your core foundation from which everything you do builds upon. Part of the problem is that methods can pervert the true intent of the Manifesto, and I will unpack that more later on.

"I really am coming to think that software developers of all stripes should have no adherence to any 'Agile' method of any kind. As those methods manifest on the ground, they are far too commonly the enemy of good software development rather than its friend. However, the values and principles of the Manifesto…still offer the best way I know to build software, and based on my long and varied experience, I'd follow those values and principles no matter what method the larger organization used."[4]
– Ron Jeffries, co-author, Agile Manifesto

Given the importance of the Agile Manifesto, I will briefly cover the intent of each value along with the corresponding principles from the Manifesto. Being Agile is a methodology-independent pursuit. This is not to suggest that you do not want to follow good practices and methods, but rather you do not want to be dependent upon any one fleeting trend. Read these with framework independence in mind.

The Agile Manifesto Values

"We are uncovering better ways of developing software by doing it and helping others do it. Through this work we have come to value:

Individuals and interactions over processes and tools
Working software over comprehensive documentation
Customer collaboration over contract negotiation
Responding to change over following a plan

This is, while there is value in the items on the right, we value the items on the left more."

Trust / Value People More Than Processes and Tools

The Agile Manifesto suggests you should prefer "individuals and interactions over processes and tools."

- ❖ The Problem: Management does not trust their teams so they push and enforce standardized processes and tools, often restricting team effectiveness and efficiency.

- ❖ Desired Outcome: Teams decide the processes and tools they need to support their work rather than conforming their work to prescribed processes and tools.

The Agile Manifesto principles I believe most align with this value statement are:

- ❖ "Build projects around motivated individuals. Give them the environment and support they need, and trust them to get the job done."
- ❖ "The most efficient and effective method of conveying information to and within a development team is face-to-face conversation."
- ❖ "The best architectures, requirements, and designs emerge from self-organizing teams."
- ❖ "At regular intervals, the team reflects on how to become more effective, then tunes and adjusts its behavior accordingly."

"It doesn't make sense to hire smart people and tell them what to do." – Steve Jobs, co-founder of Apple

---

Organizations hire smart people to solve difficult problems, yet often tie their hands by telling them how to do their work. Perhaps organizations are thinking about economies of scale – to leverage the same training and tools. Maybe, but in knowledge work, this *"need"* to command and control how work is done suggests a lack of trust and hinders a team's ability to work together to meet the needs placed before them. Software is knowledge work, not something that can be standardized like factory production. These processes become a way to control everything in a standardized way, which is not aligned with Agile at all, and not effective either.

Processes and tools have a place within your teams and should correspond to the size of the team and location of its members. Done well, processes and tools should *support* how the team works, not *drive* how the team works. The team should first determine how it wants to work, and then find practices and tools that support it. From an Agile perspective, one-size-fits-all is an *anti-pattern* – meaning it seems like the right thing to do, but is not, and has negative consequences.

Frameworks and methodologies are themselves not Agile. Scrum, for example, can be worked consistently with Agile and it can also not be consistent with Agile. Teams can sometimes violate this Agile value as they try to follow Scrum by putting too much focus on using tools or by standardizing and enforcing how all teams do Scrum. For example, Scrum uses the Sprint Review to demo what was developed to external stakeholders. This is an example of a process deciding when and how you interact.

Sometimes tools are chosen first, which then influences the processes in order to fit the tools. For example, a team might decide it needs to use Jira, a popular tool used by *"Agile teams."* This leads to processes being determined by what the tool can and cannot do. The processes followed, and how, are adopted by the team because that is how the tool works. Rather than a framework that guides, what the organization implements is a step-by-step prescription that may not be optimal for every team.

Agile promotes a people-first approach to work and trusts the ones doing the work to know how best to deliver the work. This is not to say that the team can always proceed to become Agile on their own – that they do not need a coach. Coaching is valuable, but coaching is not mandating; it is not standardizing. Coaching helps teams navigate the values and principles and to apply them to their unique situation while leveraging what works best from across many Agile methods to best live out the values and principles.

Deliver More Value, More Often

The Agile Manifesto suggests you should prefer "working software over comprehensive documentation."

- ❖ The Problem: Traditional projects require extensive documentation up front before any work begins. Experience and learning is delayed – missed value.

- ❖ Desired Outcome: Deliver something early and often so that users can experience it, the team can learn from feedback, and adjust to make a better product.

The Agile Manifesto principles I believe most align with this value statement are:

- ❖ "Our highest priority is to satisfy the customer through early and continuous delivery of valuable software."

- ❖ "Deliver working software frequently, from a couple of weeks to a couple of months, with a preference to the shorter timescale."

- ❖ "Working software is the primary measure of progress."

- ❖ "Simplicity – the art of maximizing the amount of work not done – is essential."

The traditional project mindset follows the idiom that says you should "measure twice and cut once." The result is months of defining detailed requirements and design, looking to improve confidence, before a single line of code is written.

I have yet to meet users and stakeholders that know everything they want, in detail, up front before seeing and touching anything. In my experience, the extra time and effort spent up front never produces a better product in the end compared to an *empirical approach* of inspect and adapt.

Traditional mindsets also measure success by how many of those up-front requirements are completed in a given time period. Being *"on time"* is important from this perspective. It unfortunately is still a key success measure in many organizations *"pursuing"* Agile. Agile principles suggest that success is measured by how much working software makes its way into users' hands, how frequently, and how valuable. There is a focus on customer satisfaction, which often gets overlooked in success metrics. I will unpack success measures in detail in Chapter Ten.

Although documentation is still important, the focus of the team needs to be more on starting and finishing small increments of work, and putting the highest value work into the hands of users sooner rather than later. An empirical approach will always produce a better product and reduce risk.

An empirical approach is the heart of Agile – to inspect and adapt. The ultimate validation of value delivered is feedback. That only comes by delivering something to users. No matter how smart your team is, it cannot know everything users want or need up front. Sometimes you will not know what the right thing to do is until you get started. Therefore, it is imperative to deliver something early and often and use feedback to improve. *"Maximizing the amount of work not done"* keeps the team focused on small, high-value targets for feedback.

"Early and often" alone do not make you Agile. After all, it is possible for your team to deliver things early and often, but not deliver the highest value possible, not empower teams, nor adapt well to change. Whether or not you are aligned with Agile depends on your why – why are you delivering early and often? I will explore the *common why* of organizations in Chapter Four, which you will want to avoid emulating.

Bridge the Gap Between Business and Development

The Agile Manifesto suggests you should prefer "customer collaboration over contract negotiation."

- ❖ The Problem: Business and development teams have historically been *"us versus them"* relationships. Contracts were created out of distrust and the focus is on contract adherence rather than the best solutions.

- ❖ Desired Outcome: Business and development work as one team, collaborating on doing what is necessary to deliver the right things rather than the promised things.

The Agile Manifesto principles I believe most align with this value statement are:

- ❖ "Welcome changing requirements, even late in development. Agile processes harness change for the customer's competitive advantage."

- ❖ "Business people and developers must work together daily throughout the project."

- ❖ "Agile processes promote sustainable development. The sponsors, developers, and users should be able to maintain a constant pace indefinitely."

Contracts are often about *being right* and holding providers accountable to what they said they would deliver when and how they said it would be delivered. Lack of trust is the issue and it creates an *"us versus them"* relationship. This approach removes any hope of building empirically, meaning you are restricted from delivering something small, allowing users time to experience it, learning from that experience, and then adjusting.

Adjusting simply is not built into the contract because that, by nature, changes scope. More time is often spent documenting contract adherence than simply working together to find the right solutions and dealing with the realities of complex software development.

"The whole point of agile is to combine across these different areas. The lowliest, juniorest programmer… should be connected to people who are out there thinking about the business issues and business strategies of the group that they're working with."[5]
– Martin Fowler, co-author, Agile Manifesto

Better outcomes occur when the customer and provider are working as one team striving for the same goal – to do the right work and chase value, whatever that is – and are willing to welcome changing requirements and outcomes as a result. It is an understanding that no one knows everything up front and we learn as we go, which produces the need for changes, good changes, that produce a better outcome. Contracts are still needed, but rather than rigid instruments to control, they should support the opportunity to change course as needed through customer collaboration and learning.

Contracts also should support working at a realistic and sustainable pace. Most timelines, or deadlines, are arbitrary and not based on the realities of knowledge work. Regardless, a team can only do so much and still maintain quality. Projections need to be based on actual trends, not set before.

Traditional project management fails to consistently predict when all the work will be done, and that is after extensive analysis and fixing the scope. Approaching work with an empirical intent makes the concept of *"on time"* obsolete. The team should be chasing value based on iterative feedback, not marching toward pre-planned work breakdowns.

Respond to Change – Chase Value

The Agile Manifesto suggests you should prefer "responding to change over following a plan."

❖ The Problem: Traditional projects lock in scope and track success based on how well the team meets that pre-planned scope. Change, if it happens, is not a result of an empirical approach.

❖ Desired Outcome: The team is willing and able to pivot at any time to chase value – to do the next right thing. Success is measured by value delivered, and what is learned through iteration, not by following plans.

The Agile Manifesto principles I believe most align with this value statement are:

❖ "Welcome changing requirements, even late in development. Agile processes harness change for the customer's competitive advantage."

❖ "Continuous attention to technical excellence and good design enhances agility."

The idea here is that delivering the next right thing is more important than delivering the next thing in the plan. However, traditional projects do not benefit from an empirical approach because nothing is delivered from which to experience and learn – or I should say in a manner timely enough to make a difference.

With an eye of delivering everything planned up front, even Scrum teams can form long-term project plans and merely use short iterations as measuring sticks for progress against the plan rather than to inspect and adapt. Teams that are focused on working through a pre-planned scope list without taking the time to inspect, get feedback, and change in response to that feedback are *feature factories* – mindlessly producing software but not working consistently with Agile values and principles.

Agile acknowledges that your team cannot know everything up front. The more unique and complex a project, the less the team knows up front and the more you can guarantee that change will occur, or *should* occur, in order to do the next right thing and deliver the most value. So, Agile minds not only value responding to change, they see it as mandatory for project success.

The entire Manifesto indirectly supports responding to change. Teams can respond more effectively when they interact and collaborate more often. Delivering something early and often facilitates feedback loops. Building architectures and good design allows changes to applications in small batches. These are, in essence, every value and principle of the Agile Manifesto.

The Manifesto Summarized

What are the Agile Manifesto values and principles really trying to accomplish? Did you see anything that suggests teams need to deliver more features, faster; that teams need to accurately predict what it will deliver; or that success is measured by delivering on pre-planned promises? I hope your answer is "no" because these things are not there.

Agile is about bringing the business and developers together as one team and trusting those who do the work to pursue the right things. This is accomplished by focusing on an empirical approach of *do, experience, learn, and adjust* rather than marching toward detailed plans. This is accomplished by delivering smaller batches of work more frequently so that inspection can occur, feedback can inform, and the entire team can adjust as needed to chase value. Agile is the mindset that leads to the activities needed to work empirically.

Agile = An Empirical Approach

Agile, the way of working that aligns with the values and principles of the Agile Manifesto, is at its most foundational purpose a way to be empirical in your work. This is not the scientific meaning of empiricism, but rather that an empirical approach to developing software is the heart of Agile because it constantly seeks to do something small, experience it, learn from it, and adjust as needed.

Why is an empirical approach so central to Agile? An empirical approach creates better products with less risk. What exactly is a *better* product? Is it one with the most features and capabilities? Is it one with the most advanced technology? Perhaps both. Perhaps neither.

Can you think of a software application in which you probably only use less than half of its features? Meanwhile, something you do in that software on a regular basis is lacking and you wish it better met your needs?

Too many products in use today have too many features that are rarely used or fail to meet users' needs. Traditional project thinking has us imagining all the possible capabilities users might want, and our teams go to work like factories pumping out new features. We end up developing features many users really do not want or need because teams are focused on working through a pre-planned requirements list rather than iterating and discovering. The Agile Manifesto principle *"Simplicity – the art of maximizing the amount of work not done – is essential"* is central to this idea. What is not done is many times just as important as what is done.

The Agile Manifesto made "Agile" mainstream, but the idea behind iterative development pre-dates the Manifesto by many years. This is the primary reason Agile promotes smaller and more frequent delivery. To me, Agile's core is about supporting an empirical approach to developing better solutions.

An empirical approach in software development is iterative and incremental with an eye on using real-time feedback to determine what to do next. It is important to distinguish between frequent iterations, often synonymous with a short time box (e.g. Sprint), and *iterating*, which means adjusting based on feedback. Teams can work in small batches and deliver working software frequently, but not actually *iterate*, or empirically develop.

Despite the early confidence I have seen in new projects, the reality is users tend to know more about what they want, and do not want, *after* using an application. That experiential feedback informs changes that bring the application closer to their wants and needs.

The smaller your iterations, the more frequent your feedback and the more responsive you can be to your users' needs. Feedback informs the next right thing – it continuously moves the most valuable work to the top of your list. This is the essence of Agile, of organizational agility – to do the right things more effectively and efficiently.

Nowhere within an empirical approach is the objective to deliver more work, to deliver promises, or to even have schedule predictability. The goal is to deliver value early and often to gain feedback for iteration.

It is a simple concept that by delivering smaller pieces of functionality early and often, you have the opportunity to empirically learn. This gives your users the opportunity to experience the deliverable, provide feedback, and inform necessary adjustments you could never have anticipated at the beginning of the project. With this approach, the end product will be different than anything you could have predicted without this feedback loop. The outcome will always be a more refined product that better meets the needs of your primary users.

A Metaphorical Example

Problem/Opportunity: Your stakeholders need a faster way to get from here to there than walking.

To help demonstrate how an empirical approach delivers a better product, consider this metaphorical example. Your stakeholders provide you with a vague need to be able to get from here to there faster than walking. Similar to many software development projects, the users have an idea of the problem they are trying to solve and what they may want, but discovery eventually reveals what is really needed. Two teams will work separately in this example to try and meet the need.

Team One decides that a car is the way to go and begins producing a car. The team uses Scrum and performs all the ceremonies such as Sprint Planning, Sprint Review, Retrospectives, and Daily Scrums. Of course, the way cars are built, it is impossible to deliver anything the user can try and use until the whole thing is complete. The team divides out the work tasks into Sprints and shows the stakeholders what was done each Sprint. Perhaps the stakeholders can provide feedback on the chassis, body, engine, transmission, electronics, paint, and such as the team gets to those capabilities, but it cannot actually use the car until the end.

Team Two, however, takes this request and quickly produces a skateboard, and gives it to the stakeholders. The stakeholders like that the skateboard is faster than walking, but it is too much effort to balance, and navigating curbs requires bending down to pick up the skateboard. It meets the initial ask, but quickly is found to not be what is desired.

Team Two uses that feedback and adds a handle, turning it into a scooter. This solves the balance issue as there is something to hold on to, and the extended handle allows the user to manipulate it much easier.

Earlier usage was on smooth surfaces, so it was not a known issue before, but the users now recognize that the scooter's wheels do not roll over pebbles and rough surfaces well. They also decide that going a little faster is ideal. The team then produces a bicycle. The stakeholders like how it more smoothly goes over the terrain, they can sit, it is much faster, and it requires less work on their part to propel the vehicle. An added benefit of this iteration is that they can coast for longer distances.

At this point, it is very feasible that the stakeholders agree this is good enough, at least for now, and redirects the team toward some other more pressing problem to solve. They may decide that the incremental value of tweaking this idea is less valuable than starting to address another problem.

The stakeholders working with Team One have not had anything to experience and only have a vision of what the end product might provide, some day. They may have received status updates and talked about the seats for the car, but have not been able to provide tangible feedback to help reach the right product. Meanwhile, Team Two is helping the stakeholder work with a *Minimum Viable Product (MVP)* – the simplest complete solution to meet the problem.

Minimum Viable Product (MVP) – key word is "viable"

Let us take this example even further. As it turns out, the stakeholders eventually decide that they would rather not have to work so hard pedaling a bicycle, so Team Two goes back to work and produces a motorcycle. Much better, the stakeholders say. They like still being exposed to the sunshine, it is fast, fairly comfortable, and less effort. However, they are now thinking they would rather not have to balance it (it is too heavy) as it can too easily fall over and is extremely hard to pick up again. This is something the stakeholders would not have known up front without having experienced it.

Team Two iterates once again and produces a trike, or a three-wheeled motorcycle. This solves the problem of balance and falling over, while maintaining all the features the stakeholders previously liked. Now the stakeholders use this for a while, but later decide that the only problem is weather. When it is cold or rainy, the trike is not very handy, but they otherwise love the open-air concept. So, the team produces a car, but a convertible. Perfect. The stakeholders still have the exposure to the sunshine but can close the top if it is cold or raining, it is very comfortable and fast, and it meets all the current needs.

In the end, Team One and Team Two may have both produced a car, but which team produced the better solution? Team Two produced the better solution because it learned along the way that the stakeholders enjoyed being exposed to the good weather, thus they produced a convertible. Additionally, which team provided the most value along the way? Team Two produced the most value along the way because each iteration provided a deliverable that was used for a time. Team One only provided value upon delivering the entire car – which ultimately was not what the stakeholders wanted.

The point of this example is to demonstrate how delivering something minimal in short cycles provides the feedback to produce a better overall product in the end. The less confidence you have up front about what is needed, the more valuable an empirical approach is. What may be even more effective about this example is that it demonstrates how early renditions (e.g. bicycle) can potentially produce just enough to solve the problem at hand today so the team can refocus its efforts on the next right thing. This is the heart of Agile.

Agile = a Foundational Mindset

An empirical approach is a timeless method to developing the most appropriate solutions with the least risk. The Agile Manifesto is a timeless set of values and principles that help guide teams toward working empirically. Those foundational layers are about mindset – what you believe, not how you do it. As the diagram below demonstrates, what you do, your practices, will come and go, but need to align with the values and principles to allow you to work empirically. If that alignment is not there, you are not Agile.

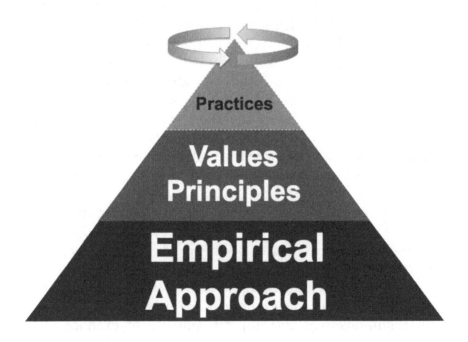

Intended Purpose of Agile

In Chapter Four, I provide you with the popular reasons why organizations choose Agile. I spend a chapter dissecting these reasons to give you perspective – that there is a disconnect between reality and *"common wisdom."*

Organizations flock to Agile for the promise of faster delivery and more predictability. Those benefits are definitively possible following Agile – just maybe in different ways than commonly thought. This incomplete view of the intent of Agile prevents organizations from achieving all that Agile offers.

An incomplete interpretation can still lead to some success, but will it lead to the outcome you desire?

Organizations have always wanted to deliver faster, and the Agile Manifesto *seems* to support that objective. Agile does support shorter cycles with smaller deliverables that facilitates the ability to deploy something more frequently. However, the idea that Agile is about doing more, faster, is incomplete.

The question to answer and understand is *why does Agile promote smaller units of work delivered more frequently?* Embracing the intended purpose of Agile will set your mind on a different, more aligned course.

Better Products

Agile is ultimately about better products.

Value People

Better products result from valuing and empowering your people. It is people interacting and collaborating that determines the next right thing to do and how best to do it. It is people that are closest to the work, closest to the product, closest to the users that make the best decisions.

Agile intends to solve the problem of developers being treated like commodities that merely bang out code to produce what others say is the best thing to do and how best to do it. Agile intends to bridge the gap between the business and development to create a more unified team.

An empirical approach should naturally bring people together more frequently as small deliverables are used, input is provided, lessons are learned, and the team collaborates on what the next right thing is. This collaboration also informs the team how to better deliver the solution next time.

Learning to empower the teams is a cultural shift for many organizations, but necessary to benefit from the intentions of Agile and to benefit from the value of the smart people the organization hires.

Inspect and Adapt

Better products result from frequent inspection and adaptation of both the product and the team's process. An empirical approach works for both cases and is the heart of Agile.

From a product perspective, small deliverables of working software give users early opportunities to experience the capabilities, to provide feedback, and help inform the next right thing. This frequent input leads to a better overall product.

From a team process perspective, frequent inspection of the team's practices allows the team to identify and improve regularly, which helps the team produce better outcomes.

Provide Flexibility

Better products result from flexibility. The best way to handle uniqueness and complexity is through short iterations of do, experience, learn, and adjust. Keep in mind that any adjustment that is made as a result of the learning you gain through experiencing the outputs is inevitably going to lead to a divergence from the original plan around scope, requirements, or presumed solution. When that happens, the next right thing can only be achieved if one gives up the preconceived plan. Therefore, allowing the finished product to be different than the planned product is an absolute must if you move to Agile thinking and approaches.

Any hard deadline is going to force certain requirements off the table simply because it is not feasible to get more done than time will allow. No matter how much overtime the team works, no matter how many people you throw at it, there is only so much a team can produce. When that wall is hit, and not all of the requirements can be delivered by the deadline, scope decisions still need to be made regardless of which approach you take – some flexibility is still required.

Reduce Risk

Better products result from reducing risk exposure. Nothing is more risky than an all-or-nothing deployment of a large application, or many varied changes in a major release. Agile, and the practice of smaller iterations, reduces risk by limiting how much change is introduced to an application at any given time, and by allowing the next update to be just a short time away. With fewer changes at any one time, there is less opportunity to break something or head down the wrong path. If either does happen, there is less risk of not knowing the cause of why something broke.

The more complex a project, the riskier it is, thus the more Agile is an appropriate fit. Complexity and uniqueness play off each other, so I will speak to these together. Something might be complex simply because it is the first time the team has taken on the specific task, or it has been a long time since they have last performed that specific type of task. Therefore, its uniqueness injects some level of complexity.

If you have ever loaded new string into a weed trimmer, you will know exactly what I am talking about. Loading new string is not rocket science, but for someone who has never done it, it can seem like it is. The first time is encumbered with lots of reading and looking it over, then laden with mistakes, before you finally get it right. Or am I only speaking for myself? For me, by the time it needs changed again, I have forgotten vital lessons learned since the last time I performed the task. Or maybe you can relate more to making a certain meal or dessert. Whatever the task, the first time is slowest, with more mistakes, so uniqueness adds to complexity.

Complex problems and complex solutions come with much uncertainty. The more complex a project, the less confidence we actually have up front about what we will ultimately end up producing, especially within a given timeline. We often find out what we can and cannot do, or what is the best solution, *after* we are waist deep in the project. This naturally requires changing direction to some degree to account for the learning that happens along the way. As a result, empirical iterations are ideal when there is a high degree of complexity.

Users often do not know what they want until they see it, or the team is not sure if their ideas will work until it is proven out through at least a prototype. This up-front uncertainty adds some level of complexity to any project because the team has to deliver against subjective criterion that empirically evolves. This is why an empirical approach works so well in the first place.

Agile practices allow the biggest risks to be pushed forward and dealt with early in the process. If an idea is not going to work as expected, Agile practices allow the team to determine that early, and adjust. Betting wrong on technical or functional needs is less impactful when addressed in small, empirical cycles. As a result, the team can try more things with less fear, further supporting the ability to deliver better products.

Increase Quality

Better products result from increased quality. Trying to keep a traditional project on schedule while maintaining fixed scope usually requires cutting corners somewhere. To maintain fixed scope within the fixed timeline, those projects often sacrifice quality. Agile promotes a fixed standard of quality.

In Agile, time and cost are often fixed and scope is variable. Since scope is variable, quality standards are able to remain fixed. The team produces to that quality standard within the time and cost allotted and delivers as much value as possible within those constraints. You may not get everything you hoped for in the time box, but you should get everything at the same high quality.

Methodologies have included automated testing to ensure continuous testing with every code check-in. Issues are found and corrected very quickly. Agile methods provide more testing and validation, more frequently, across smaller portions of the solution, which in turn promotes higher quality.

Chapter 2:
Timeless Concepts

The Agile Manifesto became an agreed upon way of thinking, or an approach to work, that was (and is) methodology independent. This not only leads to various practices, but there are also other thought processes or concepts that match well with these values and principles.

Agile Transformation

Aligning the way your organization *thinks*, mind by mind, to effect a change in organizational behavior.

In this chapter, I will summarize a few key concepts that, combined with the Agile Manifesto, build the foundation for your Agile transformation.

I believe these concepts apply across any organization, in any industry. How you live out these concepts in practice can vary. Popular methodologies certainly incorporate these concepts, or at least you can get there by borrowing from a few of those methodologies. In the end, transformation is mind by mind – mindsets not methods. Embracing these concepts is foundational to having a better *why* behind your what.

Empirical Approach

The empirical approach concept was covered at great length in the previous chapter, but the importance of embracing this as the core of everything you do cannot be overstated. Getting into a routine of doing something, providing it to stakeholders to experience, learning from that experience, and then adjusting is critical to living out Agile.

You may not consider Agile as an applicable approach to car manufacturing because it all seems well understood and routine. Granted, a production line for a car manufacturer is not using an empirical approach to mass-produce cars. They may be using Kanban to optimize flow, but the process of *do, experience, learn, and adjust* definitely is used during design and prototyping in order to get to that first production-ready model. Furthermore, it is used continuously to gain feedback from current customers, which feeds improvements into the next model update. If you look at any mass-produced product you will see that an empirical approach is used in design and prototyping in order to better know what customers want. The actual production process takes on a different methodology.

If your organization produces a software application product, how you build and grow that application may take on one approach, how you go about integrating it and customizing it for clients may use a different approach, and how you support it yet another. Regardless, you should always be looking to get user feedback from which to inform future enhancements. That is an empirical approach. I assume your organization produces a product or provides a service and, whether you have thought about it before or not, you are likely using an empirical approach in some manner. The question is, are you doing that consciously and effectively?

When it comes to cutting edge or new product ideas, there simply is no way to guess what users want or need in great detail or how it will evolve. Sure, you can know to a certain degree what users want and need, but you cannot know every possible requirement or predict how users will want the product to evolve.

Any project being done for the first time, or a variation of something not done that way before, cannot be planned fully up front. Projects that are complex and not well understood up front (i.e. every custom software project, television commercial, home remodel) cannot be worked out according to a strict work breakdown schedule. Sure, each of these things may have been done before, but not exactly like what the team is embarking on this time around. Feedback informs changes. Risks materialize, which necessitate changes. This is why an empirical approach truly fits so many organizations, perhaps more than you might expect.

Agile-minded methods are about breaking work down into smaller, more manageable chunks that are independent from all other work. In other words, these smaller units of work have end-to-end value and can be deployed and used immediately through short development cycles.

Early and continuous delivery allows for an empirical approach. The basic premise is that when trying to plan large amounts of requirements up front, what you deliver is usually wrong – you will likely miss the mark in some way. You also know the least amount about a project and its best solution early on – it is mostly theory. Therefore, biting off smaller chunks and getting the solutions into the hands of users allows you to learn from their experience and make appropriate adjustments. This incremental process not only reduces risk, but it produces a product down the road that benefits from continuous feedback, which is always a better product.

In the following sections, I will unpack individual concepts that all tie back to supporting an empirical approach. These concepts also support each other. When melded together with the Agile Manifesto, you have what you need to walk the path toward a lasting Agile transformation.

Minimum Viable Product (MVP)

It is no coincidence that one concept overlays another. An empirical approach and minimum viable product are tightly woven, and you will continue to see these and other concepts build upon one another as you move through this chapter.

If you have any exposure to Agile, you have likely heard the term *minimum viable product,* or MVP. Some may also call it minimum marketable product or minimum marketable feature. In other words, it is the minimum solution you can deliver to meet the requirement or goal. Liken this back to my previous example in Chapter One regarding a better way to get from here to there – a bicycle is perhaps a lesser solution than a car, but it may very well be adequate enough to meet the need. This is the perfect compliment to an empirical approach.

Perhaps you have been told all your life that you must go above and beyond and exceed expectations. Is that really the right thing to do? From both a Lean and Agile perspective, going above and beyond, or exceeding expectations, is wasteful. If this is a hard pill to swallow right now, that is understandable, but it is a pill you must learn to swallow to maximize effectiveness and efficiency in delivering the highest value for your stakeholders.

The word *minimum* may throw you off because you may have been taught that the minimum really is not good enough. Keep in mind that *minimum* here is relative. How much you build out a feature depends on the product, the organization, and the market or environment the product is used in.

It is important to understand that the key word here is *viable.* By definition, viable means it is capable of working successfully. With respect to MVP, it means it meets the requirement. Therefore, a minimum viable product fully meets the requirement, but no more. Why is this an important concept to embrace?

When producing anything, you will touch on a concept called the *Theory of Diminishing Returns*, or the *Law of Diminishing Returns*. As the following chart shows, the greatest value delivered in any project occurs in the earlier phases of the effort. Once the MVP is attained, the incremental value available diminishes compared to the effort required.

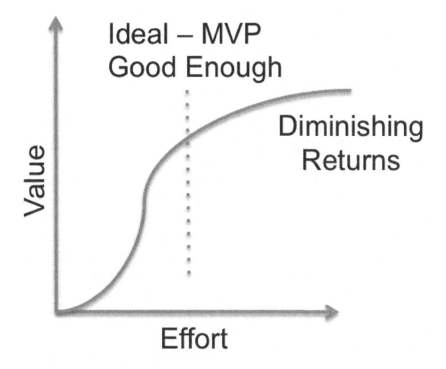

Ultimately the decision is this – is the additional value you can provide by going above and beyond on one thing greater than the value you could provide by putting time and resources into starting a different task, or project? Is that user interface enhancement for an existing feature more important than implementing the next product feature that does not yet exist? Only you and your stakeholders can make that value decision. If you are truly going to find success with Agile, MVP is a concept your organization *must* embrace.

The term *barely sufficient* is similar to MVP, but tends to be used regarding documentation. It carries many of the same characteristics – document only what is needed, when it is needed. Similar to the MVP concept where *viable* was the key word, the key word in this case is *sufficient.* Sufficient means good enough. It meets the need, it provides value, and so the *Law of Diminishing Returns* applies to documentation as well.

The key to documentation is that what you document must be useful, not just now, but later. If people do not use the documents, or do not use sections of the documents, why create the content? Only document what you need when you need it, just enough to convey the meaning. Pictures are worth a thousand words. Start with what you know and progressively elaborate. Barely sufficient is the goal.

Let us walk through this with an example. You are building a new mobile application that will allow consumers to find local restaurants. Some ideas around "find restaurants" include providing an alphabetized list, and search by name or food type. Another idea is to find local restaurants based on GPS location of the device used. Other ideas for features include the ability to reserve a table, to allow consumers to read and write reviews for the restaurants, and to see menus. Additional considerations may be that to reserve a table, you could provide users with the restaurant's phone number or you could provide a form to fill out that sends a reservation request to the restaurant. To submit reviews, it could be done anonymously or require an account. If there is an account, should there be member's only content and features? To provide menus, should it be a document or page content, and should the restaurant have a way to update this content through some administrative portal? This list could go on.

It is common to have a natural desire to implement the most amazing features, and all of them, in version 1.0. That thinking leads to detailed requirements documents defining explicit details. That simply is not prudent, and many times not feasible due to technical, time, and/or cost constraints. Therefore, hard decisions need to be made. In making priority decisions, MVP comes into play, not just for the product as a whole, but for feature sets as well. What is the minimum problem you need to solve right now, and thus what is the minimum feature set you need to launch in the first version of the application? What is the minimum documentation needed to convey the ideas to get started?

If you are in a race with a competitor to be the first to market, how does that impact your decision? For example, is it more important to have GPS location search now or have the ability to reserve a table through the application, and then do GPS in a later version? Is a simple list or simple search good enough for now so that you can provide some basic reservation capability early, or is enhanced search more important than having any reservation capability at all right now?

These are the types of value trade-off decisions your product team needs to consider. To help with those decisions, basic mockups of screen design and flow might help stakeholders visualize ideas. Hand-drawn design diagrams might suffice to help the team understand the complexities. Detailed documentation of what you delivered is far more valuable than details of what you *might* deliver. Keeping the team focused on MVP, with *sufficient* documentation, is an effective way to navigate the value proposition so your team is delivering the next right thing.

Speaking of the next right thing, this becomes your natural focus when your team is always prioritizing each feature and enhancement based on its *individual value*. The team becomes value-driven, which is our next core concept.

Value-driven

It seems reasonable to think that all organizations are focused on delivering the highest value at all times. I genuinely believe that decision makers desire to provide value, and that they are convinced they are doing so. However, the observable actions do not always support that notion.

What does value-driven mean? Is not everything you do valuable? It may come as a shock to you, but not everything you do each day, not everything your team produces, is valuable – or at least is not the *most* valuable thing you could have done. I admit, there is a bit of shock value in that claim, but I say this simply to convey, and hopefully get you to agree, that we have to redefine what value is and what it means.

The next right thing vs. the next thing in the plan.

I like to use the terms "chase value" and "the next right thing." What is valuable to your organization and your product can, and should, change fairly frequently if you are gathering stakeholder feedback and adjusting to their needs regularly. The best way to allow your organization to chase value is to ensure the team is working empirically with MVPs. These tight feedback loops can inform and provide opportunities for changing direction as needed. Plan to re-plan, and always look to do the next right thing – chase value not milestones.

Think about a traditional project where you define requirements up front and then work toward delivering all of them. These requirements are usually built out in some sequence. Furthermore, no one can seem to imagine a solution without all those features being delivered, together. I say *"traditional"* projects, but many teams are still following this all-or-nothing approach in Scrum – they are working in defined time boxes, but there is no usable value each Sprint.

Have you ever considered how the team would go about delivering those requirements if they were each prioritized by their individual value rather than by what is most convenient to develop? Can you then imagine what the product would look like if, halfway through the planned development time, you simply said pencils down? What would the team have delivered up to that point? Which approach would produce the most valuable product overall? I think that would be an interesting experiment to test with two teams doing the same small project, with one using all-or-nothing approaches and the other empirical. Surprise them halfway through and see which product is most valuable as-is.

The general premise is that you can deliver the absolute minimum capability across all functional areas of the solution, thereby having an end-to-end solution even though it may not be pretty or feature-rich. Alternatively, you can spend the same amount of time building out robust features in just one or two functional areas. Which product is most useful overall?

Case Study

Project: Build a case management system to manage a program to help ex-felons get jobs. Fixed budget project.

Challenge: Not all details of the program were known, but the program progression/flow was understood.

Strategy: Built MVPs of each module as needed and added enhancements to prior modules as priority and funds allowed. Iterative and incremental based on value.

In this case study, my team knew that the program would progress applicants from data intake through training, job placement, and then to follow-up activities. Each step in the process would need the corresponding module in the case management application. Data intake would begin in barely enough time to deliver a MVP of the intake module. The other modules would need to be delivered in quick succession.

Even if the team could have delivered each module when it was needed, going above and beyond the minimally needed capabilities too soon may have risked our ability to finish. Working with a fixed budget, we decided that it was better to get the entire application built minimally first, and then use remaining funds and time to go back and polish the application. Otherwise, the team could have run out of money before all the *necessary* features were complete.

Being value-driven and focused on MVP using an empirical approach produces a better product, but it also reduces risk. The plug could also be pulled on your project, or your priorities may be shifted. If that happens, will you have something functional and valuable, or just partial, disjointed work that can only sit on the shelf?

The example of stopping development halfway through is not just some dramatic example to prove a point – it happens. Situations arise that require teams to stop what they are doing and switch gears to something else more important. Ideally, you have, at most, a couple of week's worth of work that cannot be deployed. Everything else has either already been deployed along the way or is production-ready. Can you see how this process and approach greatly reduces risk?

The world around you changes fast, and your stakeholders' needs shift frequently. You better position yourself to act on and deliver the next right thing when you put off certain decisions and activities until *the last responsible moment*. That idea leads us to the next Lean concept.

Last Responsible Moment

You may have been scolded at some point in your life about waiting until the last minute to do something. I am now suggesting this may be a good thing and it compliments an empirical approach, MVP, and a value-driven mindset.

Decision-making presents two dilemmas: early decisions and late decisions. With early decisions, if you make them too early, you are likely to be wrong because you know the least up front, or early in the project. Being wrong means you end up producing the wrong thing and that causes rework, or failure. With late decisions, you risk missing out on opportunities, which also can cause rework or failure. The balance is the *last responsible moment*.

As you can see from the following graph, there is a cost to deciding and a cost of deferring. The last responsible moment is that intersection.

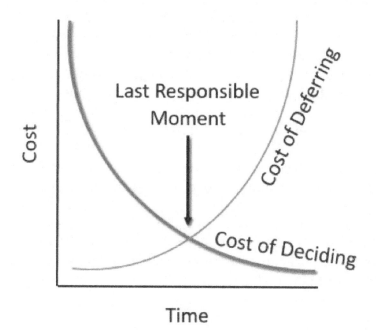

Note here that the key word is *responsible*. It ultimately comes down to this – why spend time on something that could change by the time it is needed? The risk of being wrong is highest in the beginning. Use time to your advantage to gain as much information as possible. Use an empirical approach to learn. Allow for adjustments to help you make the right decisions and put in the right effort at the most effective time.

You may have heard of the Lean-manufacturing concept of Just-In-Time (JIT), which suggests that you should only produce products when they are needed versus building up inventory. When an order is placed, the product is produced JIT versus being pulled from inventory where the product has been sitting for a time. The less time the product sits idle, the better. From a Lean perspective, inventory is waste. Inventory is not producing income, it is not providing value to users, and it takes up space that costs money. This concept applies to the solutions your team produces in similar ways.

Requirements and design work that are not ready to be used in development is inventory. Therefore, the further away a task is from needing to start, the less you should think about and work on that item. When you adhere to this concept, you resist the need to flesh out requirements for lower priority work items. Otherwise, by the time you get to those items, assuming you ever do, what is needed may have changed. Focus most on your highest priority requirements – the ones you are closest to starting.

The same goes for making decisions. The more time and effort you put into making a decision ahead of when that decision needs to be made, the more inventory you metaphorically build up. You are essentially throwing away unused inventory if anything changes along the way. When you rethink and alter previous decisions made, the time and effort previously spent may no longer be applicable to your decision.

Anything Worth Doing is Worth Doing Poorly

Between *minimum viable product* and *last responsible moment*, I have given you two very challenging concepts which may go against everything you have been taught about how to conduct business. Now I am saying that anything worth doing is worth doing poorly. If these concepts are new to you, I completely understand if your head is spinning and you are wondering how any of this can be good for business. This particular concept is a bit more nuanced, phrased in a way to be shocking, so please do not miss the point.

You should never *want* to do work poorly. In fact, Agile naturally produces a higher quality deliverable than other approaches, but quality standards are not really what this concept is about. This is more about simply not needing to have all the answers up front before you get started doing something you believe is valuable.

Have you ever been so caught up in planning and design, or what is commonly called *"analysis paralysis"*, that you failed to get started? If you do not start, you cannot experience anything, learn anything, or adjust anything.

If it is a good enough idea to spend time on, it is good enough to get started on to see if it really is a good idea.

The best way to prove out an idea is to *do something*. Start with what you know right now, define an MVP or proof of concept, use short empirical cycles, address risk early, and discover by doing. You will learn more and achieve more just getting started, even if *"poorly"* and not fully thought out, than you will by thinking about it incessantly.

Continuous Improvement

Continuous improvement is both a core concept and a great summary for all the key concepts I previously covered. In product development, minimum viable product is a natural, value-driven outcome of an empirical approach. Waiting until the last responsible moment allows the most valuable features to be delivered at the right time to meet stakeholder needs. The willingness to start and learn sooner rather than later supports an incremental approach to building the best possible product. This way of working naturally is a continuous improvement process for the product and solution you offer.

Organizations change when its people do.
Change never happens all at once – it is incremental.
Mindset transformation facilitates lasting change.

Your teams and your organization also need to focus on continuous improvement for how it conducts its work, and the process is the exact same. Small changes implemented frequently keep the team moving in the right direction. The team can focus solely on the most valuable changes and making them work well before tackling other issues. The Agile mind is always identifying areas for improvement, trying something different, and learning from the outcome. Tying back to "anything worth doing is worth doing poorly" fits here as well. You really cannot know if a process change will work well until you try it. This is why small changes are better than large changes. If something does not work well, you can quickly change and no one is hurt, no great effort is expended.

A *learning organization* is one whose culture supports trying new things, embracing the inevitable failures early, learning from experience, and continuously searching for better ways to work. If asked, would anyone in your organization say they do *not* want to be a learning organization? Probably not, but actions may say otherwise.

Standardization and *"best practice"* can be the enemy of continuous improvement. You may hold project management or Agile-related certifications. These certifications teach a standard way to work and rely on so-called best practices across various process areas. What is a best practice anyway? A best practice is a way of doing something that many in the industry have come to claim, through experience, as the best way to do a particular process or task. If Agile is all about *continuous improvement*, this begs the question, where do best practices fit in?

Best practices for living out the values and principles of Agile are a moving target. Not only should your team continuously improve and refine how it works, but also each team is different and works within its own context. Each team learns what processes and practices work best for their unique situation, and adjusts over time.

Specific frameworks tout best practices for how things should be done. Yes, certain practices may work well in most situations for most teams, but there is no one-size-fits-all solution. These defined practices are great starting points, but I caution you to not let them box you in. A best practice for my team may not be a best practice for your team. Continuous improvement is unique to each team and each organization. The key is that everyone is constantly moving forward while staying aligned with the Agile values and principles. Allowing that flexibility enables true Agile transformation.

Safety – Courage – No Fear

A command and control style of management is one where the managers tell their teams what to do, *and how*, and then measure their performance against how well they meet these expectations for how that work should be done. This style seemed to work well in the early industrial age, but as we moved into more knowledge work, this style has carried over, and it simply does not work. It is ironic that organizations pay nice salaries to smart people only to then tell them how the work should be done.

This style of management produces fear because when individuals and teams do not meet the performance standards placed upon them, they are penalized. Many times, what is measured, and how, is illogical and ineffective. Smart people have a conflict between doing what they know makes sense and doing what they are told. Often, doing the right thing leads to missing the mark on ill-advised measures of success.

When old-school managers say, "implement Agile," the conflict is compounded. The Agile Manifesto suggests that teams should feel free to try new ways of working that bode well for them rather than being told to use specific frameworks, methods, and tools. This naturally leads to ideas that do not work out, but is seen as failure to old-school thinkers, which leads to discipline. Worse, it leads to standardization efforts, which I will touch on later.

Scrum defined some values that touch on this safety requirement – courage, respect, and openness. Modern Agile[6] came along and listed one of its core principles as "Make Safety a Prerequisite." To be effective with an empirical approach, the team needs to feel safe to take small risks, find out what does not work, to not have all the answers, and to know that team performance is more important than individual performance. If a team does not feel safe, it cannot achieve the benefits of Agile, and that is on management.

Chapter 3:
What is Timeless Agility?

Timeless Agility is the outcome of a mindset that transcends methodology. It consistently allows you to effectively and efficiently identify, produce, and deliver the next right thing.

The statement above is a succinct description of Timeless Agility, but in a business culture flooded with frameworks, certifications, paradigm shifts, and buzzwords, why should you want to pursue *Timeless Agility*, and what does that entail?

Instead of another prescribed framework, tool, or methodology, Timeless Agility is a destination achieved by scaling the Agile mindset more so than scaling standardized *"best practices."* It is an organization-wide agility deeply rooted in the *true* meaning of Agile that leverages the best of common frameworks, but never relies too heavily on those trends. It is a methodology-independent approach to work. Each team is enterprise-aware yet capable of following whichever practices work best for it to deliver the next right thing within its own context. Let us unpack this further.

The Right Things, More Effectively

The bottom line objective of Timeless Agility is to always be able to do the next right thing, and then become better at delivering those right things. To be able to *always* do the right things, your organization will need to shift from solely focusing on Agile practices at the development and delivery team level and refocus on an enterprise-aware organizational agility where Mindset Transcends Methodology™.

While a popular framework such as Scrum may help teams deliver something sooner, it cannot help you determine what the next right thing is. Your team may become very good at delivering working software early and often, but if they are not delivering the *right* things, are they successful? You may argue that by doing the highest priority items in your backlog you *are* doing the right things. You might be, but keep an open mind on that point.

Empirical Approach

Short, repetitive cycles of *do, experience, learn, and adjust* that allow frequent feedback, iteration, and better solutions while reducing risk via smaller batch sizes.

Feedback from users of your product, as well as input from other stakeholders, can steer you toward the right things. Many organizations, unfortunately, fail to leverage feedback and learning for adaptation. A fallacy is thinking the next right thing is always about what an end-user interacts with, or that one businessperson (e.g. Product Owner) can represent all stakeholders adequately. Thus, in your pursuit of Timeless Agility, you must seek to be *enterprise-aware*.

Enterprise-aware

It is easy to assume your teams are delivering value, but how do you know it is the highest value? Do you have a way to identify and prioritize value across stakeholder groups in a way that ensures the biggest bang for the buck? Are you tackling the biggest problems and capturing the right opportunities? Do you have a method of defining value to begin with? I will later provide guidance on how you might do that, but for now, I just want to get you thinking.

The Scrum framework teaches you about building and prioritizing backlogs, but it does not cover how to know what to put in that backlog or what the next right thing is. Furthermore, Scrum does not accommodate, in fact *discourages*, more than one business representative to interact with the development team outside of constrained guidelines. Your team may be efficient at getting finished work out the door, but that certainly has no impact on helping you identify and decide on value. Scrum has the Product Owner role to represent the business priorities, but is that adequate – is that enterprise-aware?

The Agile Manifesto states that business people and developers should interact daily. It was Scrum that decided "business people" equals just one person[7].

The product you develop and manage will always have more stakeholders than just direct end users. Data intake may be consumed, manipulated, and processed in some manner. The application may ingest, use, or display external data. Downstream business processes, technical roadmaps, and operations can all be influenced or affected by your product.

Are each of those stakeholders included in your product development process? Are each of their concerns factored in?

The first problem your team would have if it were not enterprise-aware is that valuable input from key stakeholders would be omitted. This can happen when teams rely on the single Product Owner to listen to and convey all the technical and functional needs of all the stakeholders. This first assumes all stakeholders are consulted. Secondly, it assumes this single business representative understands the product, its technology, and the overall business enough to adequately translate those conversations into the right things to do. That is a tall order for one person, and where many teams falter.

Even when you are representing all your stakeholders, "enterprise-aware" has additional meaning. Let us assume that your development team wants to deploy some amazing new feature. If that new capability requires new data intake, have you cleared it with your privacy compliance folks? Does the new feature need security review and acceptance? Have you coordinated with marketing to plan the release messaging to ensure this amazing new feature gets the publicity and adoption rate you desire? Have you checked with your infrastructure and enterprise architecture teams to make sure the technology you want to use fits in the overall technology roadmap and can be supported? Have you and marketing discussed with support teams about how many upgrades or new users you expect, and when, so that the organization can properly support any issues that inevitably come up? As you can see, product management needs to be enterprise-aware.

Your organization might factor all these things as well as anybody. For many, however, what can happen is the development team may learn to be very effective at producing what stakeholders want, but the rest of the organization does not work to the same values and principles. The development team may be Agile, but the organization around it is not. What is needed is an organization-wide Agile transformation.

Organizational Agile Transformation

The idea of organizational agility is not new – it is merely elusive. Where you might run into trouble is that your organization may be pursuing Agile but its current approach is not leading to genuine organizational agility.

To many, Agile transformation is standardizing frameworks and practices across the organization – to change how *development teams* work across the board. Granted, the Agile Manifesto is focused on software development, but it does not suggest standardization. To these organizations, Agile transformation means that all teams are doing Scrum and are perhaps plugged into the Scaled Agile Framework® (SAFe®). The data I present in upcoming chapters demonstrates that point. However, where they go wrong is that the transformation is not rooted in the true intentions of Agile nor is it enterprise-aware.

SAFe® seems to exist to help larger organizations scale up and out to coordinate software delivery across the enterprise. This certainly sounds like an enterprise-aware approach, but I believe it is an Agile *anti-pattern.* Being enterprise-aware means incorporating non-development teams, so I recommend transforming (or scaling) something everyone needs to be aligned with – the mindset. I will discuss scaling in more detail in Chapter Nine.

Anti-pattern

A commonly used practice that initially appears to be the appropriate thing to do but has more bad consequences than good ones.

For many organizations, SAFe® provides the structure and control they are accustomed to having while being able to say they are doing Agile practices. Moving to *"Agile"* in this way is comfortable because they can avoid having to make the necessary cultural changes that Agile intends for us to make. It may scale Scrum teams and releases, but it does nothing to scale the Agile mindset, nor to propagate that way of thinking throughout the organization. The organization transforms and scales how command and control is done, but it does not transform what it believes about work.

If mindset transcends methodology,
which should you focus on scaling?

When left up to each team to determine what they should do, and how, my experience has been that separate teams will rarely collectively agree across the board on the best tactical approach. Therefore, the only way to have consistency across your processes, practices, and tools for every team is to mandate it – to force it. Experience shows that even then you will not have complete consistency because teams will usually seek out alternative ways to subvert what does not work for them. An organization committed to ensuring complete compliance across the board creates new roles for *"process hawks"* (e.g. Project Management Office) to keep alignment and adherence to these standards.

This idea to force standards across all your teams does not align with the values and principles of Agile. Following Agile should allow each team to independently determine how it can optimize to deliver the organization's priorities. Standardization may feel like the right thing to do, but it is an anti-pattern. Standardization constrains teams and it obstructs local optimization.

Forcing the "best" way onto your teams is not a sustainable model for achieving lasting organizational agility because, in the Agile mind, there is no such thing as an absolute "best practice." Achieving real Agile transformation requires changing how each mind thinks about work, which leads to learning how to live out the values and principles of Agile regardless of the environment.

Would you prefer to have everyone doing the same thing or would you prefer that each team be optimized within its own context and capability?

Organizational agility is a way of thinking and approaching work that requires more than just learning "Agile methodologies" within a development team. It is about how quickly your organization can successfully deliver the right things. Your *entire organization* plays a role in determining what the right thing is and then supporting the ability to deliver it. The entire organization would not follow the same processes and practices as your development teams. Rather than seeking to transform *how* everyone works, first transform the thinking around *why* they do what they do and why they do it a certain way. The *why* has to be aligned in order for the organization to achieve true agility.

Timeless Agility is about developing a mindset that transcends methodology; that embraces a way of working that will stand the test of time. It is about internalizing core values and principles for what to do, and why, more so than learning how to do specific practices or using specific systems which come and go anyway. The goal of Timeless Agility is to never again be at the mercy of the latest trends in methodology, paradigm shifts, or the constraints that accompany them.

Mindset Transcends Methodology

In the "Certification Economy", as I call it, there is a strong focus on learning and *doing* very specific frameworks and practices. Scrum and SAFe® offer a plethora of trainings, certifications, and coaching specific to their tools and methods. Despite allowing for some variation, frameworks, for the most part, are there to keep practices consistent.

Frameworks help teams coalesce around new ways of working. The argument can be made that structured frameworks help teams learn how to work differently by providing a consistent cadence and methodology to what they do. I cannot disagree with that. The question is, which practices are *"best"*?

A best practice is something that has been tried and proven to work for most people in most situations. The Project Management Institute maintains the Project Management Body of Knowledge (PMBOK®), which is a detailed set of best practices. The PMBOK® is a fairly stable set of practices, but it does get updated from time to time. Agile believes strongly in continuous improvement, so how much more so should the practices of teams following Agile change?

If you think you have the best way,
you likely stop looking for a better way.

Continuous improvement is a core principle of the Agile mindset, which means best practices are a moving target and represent something different to each team. What is best for one team may not be best for another, at least at any given moment in time. Do I think there are common methods that teams will gravitate to and do well with? Yes. However, each team will progress at its own pace and there is more than one *"best"* way to live out Agile. While Scrum may allow some variation, it intends to be followed rather rigidly. I prefer to be able to completely change what my teams do, and how, depending on their unique needs in that moment.

Transforming what you do and how is never ending. Transforming *why* you do what you do – how you think about work – that becomes your rock-solid foundation. Think about your business. Is it fair to suggest that your goal has always been to be able to identify, produce, and deliver the next right thing? Have you always wanted to be able to do that well? What about your methods to achieve that goal? Have they changed over the years? Hopefully the answer is "yes." This is a good thing, actually. You *should* change what you do if what you are doing is not the most effective and efficient way to do the next right thing. That is the point – your *why* outlives your *how* – Mindset Transcends Methodology™.

> Your how will come and go but your why
> should remain much more constant.

The martial arts provide a great parallel to this idea. Why do martial arts exist, what is their *why*? At the risk of my point getting lost in this generality, I hope we can agree that the common historical purpose of the martial arts is predominantly around self-defense. Given that goal, why are there tens of thousands of martial arts styles worldwide?

I regularly practiced Aikido when I was younger. It was the first and only martial art I ever practiced, so it is all I knew, but that did not stop me from believing it was a better way than other styles. Aikido's style made sense to me. It seemed ideal to learn a way to protect myself against multiple attackers using their own energy against them rather than my own strength, or to leverage pressure points and joint locks to halt an attack using very little brute force.

My allegiance to the art was not based on comparable experience with other forms. My allegiance was simply that Aikido made sense to me in theory, it looked awesome in practice, and it is what I knew. This happens frequently with Agile methodologies as well, but should it?

People will advocate for what they are vested in or comfortable with as much, if not more so, than that which they have experienced true objective success with. Without personal experience, we do not know if it is the best way; we only know that it seems like the best way.

I will never forget the time I paired up with Sensei Sakamoto of the Northern Virginia Aikikai. No matter how hard I tried to "get him", I always ended up on the ground. I would get back up and try again. After several minutes, out of breath, and sweating profusely, I realized that this much older man was not even breathing heavy. It seemed like he was doing very little to deflect my attacks, and it was true. There was no need for him to punch or kick me for I was wearing myself out in futility. That experience was humbling and demonstrated what I needed to aspire to. Similarly, when observing a team seemingly executing its Agile framework effortlessly, it is only natural to want to mimic that success – to see it as the best way.

Pure Aikido lacks any punching or kicking tactics. The goal is to deflect attackers, not be an attacker. Where possible, I learned to blend with an attacker's energy in such a way as to neutralize the attack, and thus the attacker. When the situation gets too close for comfort, Aikido provides ways to use joint locks and pressure points to break free and create separation once again. However, there is nothing in the Aikido toolkit to deal with being taken to the ground in grappling fashion. Although the goal is to never be in that situation, if Sensei Sakamoto were ever to be taken down, he would have to employ something other than pure Aikido to improvise. Likewise, when I was taught where strikes *could* be made, I was learning a variation to the practice – to fill the gaps.

As awesome as Aikido is, as much as I was in allegiance to it, adding elements of other styles helped to *fill the gaps*. This happens in our teams as well. For example, concepts from Kanban are often mixed in with the practice of Scrum – to fill some gaps. This is where the term "Scrumban" comes from.

With a continuous improvement mindset, there will always be a need to "fill the gaps." In other words, hold on to your prescribed methods loosely.

It is this idea of filling the gaps that breeds new martial arts styles. Aikido itself was created as a combination of theory and technique derived from other arts. Each martial art is either a variant of something that came before or developed from learning what did and did not work previously – to fill the gaps. Many Agile practices are borrowed, some revised, and others created new. While teams may blend other practices with Scrum, Scrum itself is also a blend of what came before it.

With thousands of years of history behind us, we learn that this combat and self-defense mindset of martial arts remained constant while the methods to achieve it changed. In other words, the mindset transcended the methodology. Agile methodologies and frameworks have much less history to demonstrate the same pattern, but thus far we have seen new frameworks evolve from older ideas and existing frameworks are evolving to stay relevant, all with the intent of providing new or better ways to *live out* Agile.

Organizations have been following this same model – to continue pursuing better ways to achieve an intended goal. Scrum proponents endorse Scrum as the best way for development teams to work. This is a methodology-*dependent* approach. Timeless Agility is a methodology-*independent* approach because experience has shown that there is no one best way. Continuous improvement demands divergence, thus the practices the teams use is not the real battle to win in Agile transformation. The real battle is transforming each mind in the organization, not just development teams, and allowing each team the freedom to *fill the gaps* while maintaining an enterprise-aware approach.

By pursuing Timeless Agility, your organization will learn to achieve and maintain its agility without being tied to fleeting trends in process or tools. It will be driven instead by core values and principles, and doing what is right for each team at each moment in time. In order to do this, your organization must undergo an organization-wide Agile transformation rooted in and supported by the *true* intentions of Agile.

You can learn framework basics, practices, and new tools in a few-day workshop, but changing mindsets across the enterprise is a longer-term endeavor best suited with support from within. The goal of this book is to help you become that transformation lead in your organization.

The next few chapters will explore why organizations choose Agile, how they *"do"* Agile, and why Agile is not Agile. You may see your own organization in these depictions. The objective is to help you identify where the masses are going wrong so that you can correct your course. The latter half of the book is my practical advice on how to move forward from where you are. Timeless Agility is a journey. Many variables will come into play. My hope is that this book will help you identify your current challenges and move you forward onto the right path.

Chapter 4:
Why Organizations Choose Agile

Your organization is either thinking about or is already pursuing Agile. Why? Your teams have likely started following a specific framework, such as Scrum or Scaled Agile Framework® (SAFe®), or a system such as Kanban. Why?

- ❖ What problem(s) are you trying to solve with Agile?

- ❖ What problem(s) are you trying to solve with your chosen framework and/or methodology?

- ❖ What are your desired outcomes?

If there is one thing that those who work with me get tired of hearing me say, it is the constant question, "what problem are we trying to solve?" I believe that before solutions and great ideas are discussed, much less pursued and implemented, the problem or opportunity needs to be well understood and defined. Far too often teams move forward with solutions to the wrong problem, or proceed with less impactful outcomes in mind, either of which may lead to wrong, or less effective, pursuits.

In the Introduction, I asked you to write down what problem you wanted to solve by reading this book? If you have not done that, I encourage you to do that now.

Make Timeless Agility Your Goal

How effectively and efficiently your organization is able to do the right things defines its organizational agility.

How well your organization is able to consistently do this despite industry changes in paradigms, frameworks, and practices is an indication of your Timeless Agility.

The obstacles that are keeping you from achieving organizational agility should be the problems you are trying to solve. Maybe you are properly locked in on those problems and are going through the natural maturity progressions, but experience and data show many organizations are pursuing Agile and various practices for other reasons. Maybe not so much *other* reasons, but more so that they *think* what they are doing is the transformational path to agility – but it is not.

"So that's our current battle…it's realizing that a lot of what people are doing and calling agile, just isn't."
– Martin Fowler, co-author, Agile Manifesto

I hope it was not lost on you that I asked what you are trying to solve with Agile and with your chosen methodology as *separate* questions. Many of the reasons why organizations want Agile and choose a particular methodology are, I believe, based on a misunderstanding of what Agile is and the role it plays in transforming an organization. This misunderstanding leads to misapplication, which ultimately is focused on solving the wrong problems and pursuing the wrong outcomes.

To overcome or avoid these same challenges, it is crucial to make sure you fully understand what problem you are trying to solve, and *why*, by pursuing Agile or by attempting to adopt a specific methodology. More specifically, what outcomes do you want from this pursuit of Agile or from the practices you employ? Ultimately, whatever you do should be *fit for purpose* to the problem or opportunity you are addressing.

What is "Fit for Purpose"?

A term that simply means something fulfills an intended purpose.

The goal of doing anything should be that the end result meets a need. Otherwise why do it, right?

Hopefully you are starting to wonder what all this fuss is about – why am I making it sound like following Agile best practices and common wisdom is potentially problematic?

It is fairly common to find organizations doing things that appear to provide benefit – that appear to be fit for purpose – but when thought about more deeply, are missing the mark.

To help you analyze your situation, I will reveal what many other organizations are doing, and why. As you learn about these common reasons, reflect back on Chapter One to compare and contrast what industry is doing against the true meaning and intent of Agile. Use this to assess what your organization is doing to begin understanding where you align.

Common Reasons for Choosing Agile

CollabNet VersionOne conducts an annual survey generating responses from "a diverse set of organization sizes, geographic locations, roles, and industries" that focuses on the "global software development community." The latest result of that survey is in the *12th Annual State of Agile Report*[8] (the Report) released in 2018.

According to the Report, some of the "Reasons for Adopting Agile" cited by the respondents include:

- ❖ Accelerate software delivery
- ❖ Increase productivity
- ❖ Enhance delivery predictability
- ❖ Reduce project cost

According to the Report, some of the "How Success Is Measured..." responses cited by the respondents include:

- ❖ Velocity
- ❖ Budget vs. actual cost
- ❖ Planned vs. actual stories per iteration
- ❖ Estimation accuracy

Based on these responses, I conclude that the three primary objectives for organizations moving to Agile are:

- ❖ Faster delivery
- ❖ On-time delivery
- ❖ More predictability

Your organization is pursuing Agile and implementing various practices. Have you considered the reasons why? Are your reasons similar to the ones from the Report?

As you proceed through this book, the questions I want you to consider regarding the responses listed earlier are:

1. Are those objectives, or desired outcomes, solving the right problems?

2. Are those the right objectives, or desired outcomes, to pursue in the first place?

I find analogies to be helpful to explain concepts, so please consider the following metaphorical scenario.

The Problem: you have a wound (cut) that is exposed

Desired Outcome: to protect the wound

Possible Solutions: medical bandage, cast, or duct tape

A medical bandage, a cast, and duct tape all cover and protect a wound, but which one is *more* "fit for purpose?" Only the cast prevents bumping the wound. The advantage of the cast is that it prevents further damaging the wound by eliminating the possibility of bumping it, besides avoiding the pain of bumping it. Is a cast the best solution? Based on the desired outcome of "protect the wound," it probably is the best solution. The question is – is that the *right* outcome to pursue?

What if the outcome was to "facilitate healing of the wound?" After all, is not that ultimately what you really want? In that case, perhaps a cast is counter-effective since it does not allow the wound to breathe well, resulting in longer healing time or improper healing altogether.

Duct tape also does not allow the wound to breathe, and the negative downstream impacts, such as removing the tape, are devastating – likely reopening the wound when the tape is removed. That definitely does not facilitate healing.

A medical bandage is more fit for purpose when healing is the desired outcome. It allows medication to be re-applied to the wound; it allows changing the bandage without ripping open the wound; and it allows the wound to breathe – all helping with the healing process.

It is vital to know what problem you are trying to solve, but more so, what outcome you desire.

Take a look at this idea from another perspective. You hopefully saw from this analogy that the defined outcome determines the solution you choose in order to meet that outcome. In the following analogy, I want you to see how the benefits attained from a solution can be dependent upon, and limited by, your perspective.

Some people practice the martial art of Tai Chi for the exercise benefits. It provides that for sure. However, if one goes into Tai Chi solely focused on the exercise benefit, then that is all they will get out of it. One will not be able to defend themselves *effectively* using Tai Chi because it is not practiced with self-defense in mind. On the other hand, if one practices Tai Chi with self-defense as the objective, they will get the exercise benefits automatically as a byproduct.

The same thing happens with Agile frameworks. Many will pursue something like Scrum for the promise of delivering more stuff in a shorter time span. As a result, everything they focus on is about productivity – how to get more stories done each Sprint.

Following Agile, and Scrum, can certainly allow teams to deliver more in a given time period, but a focus on productivity will miss out on the primary purpose and benefit – an empirical approach – cycles of do, experience, learn, and adjust. So, like Tai Chi, the primary benefits of Agile are never realized when the primary purpose of the art is not the focus.

If faster delivery, on-time delivery, and attaining more predictability are your reasons to pursue Agile, is Agile really fit for purpose?

Your why, or your "so that", defines your desired outcomes. Your desired outcomes drive the solutions you pursue, as well as how you benefit from those solutions. Therefore, you need to make sure that you are defining the *right* desired outcomes so that you produce and benefit from the solutions that are *most* fit for purpose. Keep that in mind as I explore the common objectives cited in the Report.

Faster Delivery

Faster delivery can mean a couple of different things, so when it comes to what problem you are trying to solve, I will look at two common views of "faster delivery."

More Output

To some people, faster delivery equates to more outputs, which means more gets done in a shorter time period. The cited desire for more productivity, increased velocity, and reduced costs are an indication those respondents value more outputs. The hope is that if Agile can get more done in the same time span, then productivity will go up. Agile methods can definitely show tangible progress in efficiency, but be careful with this promise because it can be misleading. Whether or not costs go down, for example, depends on if more output is a result of more efficiency or simply putting in more hours.

❖ The Problem: behind schedule; over budget
❖ Desired Outcome: more work delivered in less time

Managers often choose metrics they are familiar with or that seem to be the right things to measure, but in an Agile context, tend not to be. The consequence of this output-focused thinking is often metrics that do not tell you the real story. This then leads to initiatives to improve those metrics, which tend to be focused on the wrong problem. I have some eye-opening examples that I will discuss in Chapter Ten regarding how to measure Agile success.

Bottom line, as I will demonstrate throughout the book, Agile never intended to increase *outputs*. All efforts to increase and track productivity, therefore, are not of Agile.

More Frequent Output

For others, faster delivery means getting something into the hands of users sooner. The respondents who cited "accelerate software delivery" seem to fit this category. It is not so much about getting more done in a time period as it is about getting something done and out the door quicker and *more frequently*.

❖ The Problem: too much time between deployments and user feedback
❖ Desired Outcome: product increments delivered more frequently

While it is possible, and in all likelihood probable, to produce more in a given time span following Agile approaches, it is not guaranteed, nor should it be the goal. What you are likely to achieve by *properly* living out Agile is smaller, more frequent deliverables that allow you to experience, learn, and adjust regularly – an empirical approach. After all, I believe the goal of organizational agility is to get the right things done, more effectively, so what better way is there to validate you are delivering the right things than to deliver them more frequently?

On-Time Delivery

Some organizations turn to Agile for the promise of delivering projects on time and on budget. It is the common motivator behind wanting Agile to produce more outputs in less time.

You can deliver everything promised, when it was promised, but still not deliver the next right thing.

- ❖ The Problem: behind schedule; over budget
- ❖ Desired Outcome: deliver what was promised when it was promised

The desire to measure planned versus actual is an indication that *"on time"* is important, as seen from the respondents of the Report. On-time delivery has always been the heart of project management, has it not – to deliver what you said you would deliver when you said you would deliver it? This sounds like the right thing to focus on, but is it really?

What do your users, customers, and/or stakeholders care the most about – whether you meet your timelines, or whether you solve their problem, meet their needs, or improve their lives in some way? I do not think these are one and the same. Fixed scope and fixed timeline projects, even Scrum Sprints, can deliver great value, but also can fail to benefit from frequent learning and adjustment. The wrong things, or less effective things, can be delivered on time.

One of Agile's values is responding to change over following fixed plans. You simply cannot respond to change *and* deliver original scope – these two concepts are at odds with each other. Once your plan changes, what does it mean to be on time? Yet *"on time"* continues to be the primary measuring stick for project success in many organizations. The questions to ask are, why is being on time so important, and if it is, is Agile the right thing to pursue in your organization?

More Predictability

The detailed schedules and work breakdowns of traditional projects, despite the massive amount of time and effort put in to manage them, miss the mark for on time and on budget. These projects are not as predictable as anyone would like. Thus, many turn to Agile for the hope of improved predictability. It is easier to predict what a team can accomplish in a two-week or one-month Sprint than for an entire ten-month project. Agile does provide a comfortable predictability, but in different ways than you may be used to.

- ❖ The Problem: not able to accurately predict schedule and cost for the project

- ❖ Desired Outcome: be able to know when remaining work can be completed and at what cost

The need to know when something will be done and how much it will cost has always been important. How much time and money it takes to produce a thing is critical information in the decision process for whether to proceed, delay, or reject a project proposal. The problem is, predictability in software development has historically been poor because knowledge work is unique.

Teams using Scrum and developing in two or four week cycles have some predictability. These teams estimate the work to be done in those short cycles and are usually fairly close to accurate. What the team will deliver in a year, however, is still unpredictable. The challenge with traditional projects that attempt to estimate all work schedules up front is not having the benefit of history. Agile approaches use the team's real and recent delivery cadence to predict what the team can expect to deliver in upcoming iterations. This provides some level of predictability, but only so much.

You can predict about how much a team will deliver by tracking its historical delivery cadence. What you cannot do is predict when specific features will be done beyond the upcoming iteration, or which will be done by a certain date. Why? If your team is genuinely chasing value, and using an empirical approach to learn and adjust, what your team ends up working on two months from now *should* be different than what you expected up front. Since a project has a defined start and stop date, and scope, this should cause you to begin questioning whether there is still a place for *"projects"* in software development.

Using the team's actual recent cadence is a great way to predict upcoming output. The data can inform when the team may complete all remaining work or how long it might take to complete a certain amount of that backlog. This method is fairly accurate. However, that all assumes nothing changes, which means the team would not be following an empirical process of do, experience, learn, and adjust – the heart of Agile.

I realize that it is not acceptable to suggest that Agile approaches provide no real long-term predictability. Your organization needs to understand what to expect. I agree with that. However, what that predictability looks like and how it is measured needs to change. I will work to develop and define that new perspective throughout this book.

Common Reasons vs. Intended Purpose

At the beginning of this chapter, I suggested that you compare and contrast the common reasons why many organizations choose Agile with the true meaning and intent of Agile as defined in Chapter One. The reasons organizations choose Agile, and how they measure success, is often at odds with the intended purpose of Agile. It is not that increasing efficiency and predictability are bad things to pursue – it is valuable – but Agile helps you discover what is more valuable as a first focus.

Agile primarily focuses on improved collaboration and the ability to change as needed. It supports an empirical approach where you do something small, experience it, learn from it, and then adjust. When you embrace an empirical approach in your product, you will uncover new things to develop that become more important than other work you expected to deliver. Therefore up-front plans change, thus the concept of *"on time"* changes. The values and principles of Agile are clearly more about ways to deliver better value than how to make teams produce more stuff in less time *(not the same thing)*, although the latter can still happen.

It is this misalignment that is keeping organizations from achieving the benefits of Agile. Perhaps it is keeping *you* from finding success in Agile. Understanding where you fit on this spectrum is an important first step.

Chapter 5:
How Organizations Do Agile

The previous chapter highlighted the common reasons why organizations choose Agile and how that conflicts with the intended purpose of Agile. As you can imagine, the common ways organizations go about *doing* Agile also conflicts with the values and principles of Agile. Purely playing the odds, chances are your teams are doing some of these common practices for similar reasons. I believe it is important to understand the popular teaching and practice around Agile, and why it may not be the most fit for purpose, so that you can self-assess your situation and adjust accordingly. In this chapter, I will explore:

❖ Common approaches to pursuing Agile

❖ Common techniques for "doing" Agile

"Our challenge...it's dealing with what I call faux-agile: agile that's just the name, but none of the practices and values in place...This is actually even worse than just pretending to do agile, it's actively using the name 'agile' against the basic principles of what we were trying to do."
- Martin Fowler, co-author, Agile Manifesto

Common Approaches to Agile

The VersionOne *12th Annual State of Agile Report* (the Report) indicates that organizations are moving to Agile in hopes to achieve faster delivery, on-time delivery, and more predictable delivery. These objectives lead organizations to pursue frameworks and practices that promise to help them achieve these desired outcomes. In this section, I will explore some of the common approaches cited in the Report.

Framework Adoption

According to the Report, some of the "Agile Methods and Practices" cited by the respondents include:

❖ Scrum – 56%

❖ Scrum/Kanban – 8%

❖ Scrun/XP – 6%

Scrum is by far the most popular framework used. As a framework, Scrum is meant to be a guide, although it does provide prescribed practices to follow – and teams do so with fervor. For some, straying beyond the Scrum Guide™ is sacrilegious and unnecessary. Obviously many believe Scrum alone is not the only way to work; otherwise 44% of respondents would not be following some variation, or something different altogether.

Scrum as intended is not necessarily bad. I think it has some aspects that are not aligned well with Agile, but for the most part, how it is used determines how good or bad it is. You just need to keep in mind that it is just one way teams pursue Agile. *"The problem isn't that Scrum isn't agile, though it isn't. The problem might be that you're not using it in an Agile fashion."*[9] – Ron Jeffries, co-author, Agile Manifesto.

As organizations want more of their teams following Agile practices, the question asked is no longer should teams do Agile, but how should they scale Agile? Organizations are now looking to standardize how every team operates. According to the Report, the two most popular "Scaling Methods and Approaches" cited by the respondents are:

- ❖ Scaled Agile Framework® (SAFe®)[10] – 29%
- ❖ Scrum of Scrums – 19%

Either way I look at it, the respondents are clearly focused on processes and tools to help them achieve their objectives for faster, on-time, and more predictable delivery.

Agile is commonly considered a *methodology* with *"best practices"* that all teams should follow consistently. When this does not happen, respondents believe adopting and scaling Agile becomes a challenge.

In the Report, "Challenges Experienced Adopting & Scaling Agile" cited by respondents provides the following challenges that directly relate to framework adherence:

- ❖ Lack of skills/experience with agile methods
- ❖ Fragmented tooling and project-related measurements
- ❖ Inconsistent processes and practices across teams

"What matters is that the team chooses its own path...for the team should not just choose the process that they follow, but they should be actively encouraged to continue to evolve it and change it as they go."
– Martin Fowler, co-author, Agile Manifesto

This focus on process is further demonstrated in the Report as the "Top 5 Tips for Success with Scaling Agile" cited by respondents includes:

- ❖ Internal Agile Coaches
- ❖ *Consistent Practices and Processes Across Teams*
- ❖ *Implementation of a Common Tool Across Teams*
- ❖ External Agile Consultants or Trainers
- ❖ Executive Sponsorship

I agree with the first, fourth, and fifth – it is the second and third bullets that highlight the issue. These responses demonstrate a popular focus on processes and tools, common or standardized processes and tools, which is not Agile.

You may be thinking, what is wrong with wanting consistent processes and practices, and being good at using them? Has not the software industry always sought after best practices and standards, and created certification programs around them? The Project Management Body of Knowledge (PMBOK®), Information Technology Infrastructure Library (ITIL®), and the Capability Maturity Model Integration (CMMI®) might come to mind. Is it not these standards that we all applied to *"traditional"* projects that is the crux of the pain for which we seek our refuge in Agile in the first place?

Delivery Team Optimization

You may have discovered, through your own experience, that your development teams can learn how to improve their delivery throughput by using Scrum, or some other method. Getting those solutions into the hands of real users is a whole other problem to solve. Security requirements, independent testing, configuration management policies, and compliance can be a bottleneck to a development team delivering early and often. Any desire to get small changes into the hands of users frequently for feedback and adjustment is stifled by a part of the organizational system that is not working from the same mindset, nor aligned to your development team's process or objectives.

The rise of DevOps and DevSecOps, which is shorthand for bringing together development, security, and operations functions, acknowledges and addresses the need to work more closely together to meet the desire to deploy solutions faster and more frequently. However, developing solutions faster and having a stockpile of "potentially shippable" software does not put value into the hands of your stakeholders. Deploying software is the only way to actually deliver the value. Thus, DevOps has been a necessary advancement to help organizations live out the principles for delivering value more frequently to stakeholders.

According to the Report, the pursuit of "DevOps Initiatives" cited by the respondents include:

❖ DevOps currently underway – 48%

❖ DevOps planned within the next 12 months – 23%

DevOps is merely a way of thinking and doing, supported by tools, that helps to achieve and live out the values and principles of Agile – it is itself not Agile. DevOps is not even a methodology – it is an approach to work supported by tools that facilitates testing and deploying at whatever pace the organization desires.

Think about it, a DevOps pipeline can technically support automated testing and deployments in a once-a-year *"waterfall"* deployment cycle. The difference is the frequency of production deployments, which is first driven by Agile values and principles for shorter iterations.

If your organization is currently benefitting from DevOps, you have the infrastructure, tools, and policies in place to automatically test and deploy solutions across all your development, testing, and production environments. Ideally, you are developing in short iterations with the ability to deploy to production much more frequently than annually. However, your Agile methodology and DevOps tools still do not guarantee that you are delivering the *right* things, or the next right thing. Scrum provides opportunities for inspection and adjustment, but far too often organizations are using that time to reflect on how to be more productive and efficient rather than how to empirically develop the product.

Deploying faster is a great objective, but how are you also ensuring that what gets deployed is the next right thing?

The trap many organizations fall into when they are fixated on optimizing delivery is focusing so much on delivering the next things in the backlog that they neglect taking the time to gather feedback on what has been delivered for iteration. Churning out feature after feature quickly is nice, but it neglects empirical feedback, which is the heart of Agile. This is where the term "feature factory" comes from. Organizations become efficient at delivering new features or new increments, like a well-run factory, but they often do not iterate – meaning they do not gather feedback, learn, and adjust what they delivered.

Common Techniques for "Doing" Agile

Scrum is the predominant framework taught and certified for how to *"do"* Agile. It is no surprise to me that seventy percent of respondents indicated Scrum, or some aspect of Scrum, is their preferred Agile method or practice. This is evident as the "Agile Techniques Employed" cited by the Report respondents include:

- ❖ Daily Standup (daily Scrum meeting) – 90%
- ❖ Sprint/Iteration Planning – 88%
  *Sprint Commitments
- ❖ Retrospectives – 85%
- ❖ Sprint/Iteration Review – 80%
- ❖ Short Iterations – 69%
- ❖ Planning Poker/Team Estimation – 65%
- ❖ Kanban – 65%
- ❖ Dedicated Customer/Product Owner – 63%

"Scrum" is often used synonymously with "Agile", so seeing these Scrum practices listed as ways of doing Agile is expected. The Kanban approach in this list is quite different, but seems to be an indication that many recognize the need to *fill the gaps*. Doing any of these practices is not necessarily bad. You have to *do* something but, before you embrace them wholeheartedly, I want you to understand them from a Timeless Agility perspective.

I will briefly assess each of these common techniques to help you understand how they align with the Agile Manifesto and to highlight the Agile anti-patterns that may result from each practice.

Daily Standup

A daily standup, or daily Scrum, is defined as a 15-minute meeting with the development team and its Product Owner. The meeting allows the team members to have both personal interaction and accountability. It is called a *standup* meeting because the idea is that people standing will not tend to prolong a meeting beyond its 15 minutes.

Teams typically discuss progress against yesterday's objectives, goals for the day, and any help one may need. Maturing teams may stop asking those three questions from each team member and focus solely on the work items in progress rather than each other's specific workload. The Product Owner is there specifically to answer questions and to hear and take action items to clear any known external obstacles the team is experiencing.

Team transparency and efficiency is the intent. The business, a la the Product Owner, has visibility into how the team is progressing and their obstacles. Teams can quickly surface and elevate issues that require resolution, be it the need for development assistance from within the team or to have an external obstacle cleared. Keeping productivity high and work flowing is key to this practice.

Agile Alignment

Daily standups target the following from the Agile Manifesto:

- ❖ Manifesto Value: "Individuals and Interactions over Processes and Tools"

- ❖ Manifesto Principle: "Business people and developers must work together daily throughout the project."

- ❖ Manifesto Principle: "The most efficient and effective method of conveying information to and within a development team is face-to-face conversation."

For teams that are not accustomed to interacting, this prescribed practice brings team members together with the business representative frequently. For teams that already interact throughout the day, this may not be necessary.

In an indirect way, increasing team interaction theoretically helps the team to identify opportunities for change and to move work closer to "working software."

Like anything, the practice needs to be valuable for the team; otherwise it becomes a waste of time and does not serve its intended purpose. If the standup meetings are effective and beneficial, do them, but do not feel obligated to do them just because they are part of a framework.

Anti-patterns

Daily standups are intended for the development team and its Product Owner to surface obstacles that need to be cleared in order to keep the flow of work moving. What can easily happen, however, is daily standups turn into rote status meetings because someone (e.g. Scrum Master) is also serving as the taskmaster.

The first problem this poses is the team tunes out what others are saying. When it feels like a status meeting, the entire meeting feels like a waste of time because team members already know what the others are doing. The intended purpose of the meeting is lost.

Another problem this poses is that a status meeting becomes an oversight mechanism for management to make sure the team is *"on time."* Teams, feeling the weight of productivity oversight, do not feel trusted or empowered. In this environment, the team's updates are more about looking good than surfacing truth. This violates the Manifesto principle "Build projects around motivated individuals. Give them the environment and support they need, and trust them to get the job done."

Sprint / Iteration Planning

In Scrum, the team holds a Sprint Planning meeting at the beginning of each Sprint. If Sprints are two weeks long, then once every two weeks the team holds a Sprint Planning meeting. This practice aims at the predictability gap, at least for the upcoming development increment.

The purpose of this meeting in Scrum is for the development team and the business to come together and review the backlog of proposed work to determine what should be done in the upcoming Sprint. In addition to deciding which backlog items to do, the team discusses them enough to understand what to do and to estimate them. With estimations in hand, the team agrees on the scope it thinks it can complete, or what it can commit to, within the Sprint.

A Sprint Planning meeting can last several hours to allow teams time to understand the proposed work. The reason so much time is needed is because most of the proposed work has not yet been vetted well by the team. This is a good thing as it aligns with the principle to "wait until the last responsible moment." Waiting until just before something needs to be acted on is the optimal time – it is just in time.

Agile Alignment

Sprint Planning indirectly targets all four values from the Agile Manifesto, as well as many of its principles. To summarize the alignment, Sprint Planning brings development and the business together for interaction and collaboration over what the team should work on next. Just enough elaboration is provided at just the right time to understand the work, to estimate its size and effort, and to feel confident about what can be delivered at the end of the Sprint.

This practice supports the opportunity to employ an empirical approach, but does not guarantee it. How the team determines value and the priority of what to work on next is not a practice that Scrum, or any other Agile methodology provides guidance on specifically. The team must look elsewhere to learn how to do that effectively. Chapter Ten on measuring success will provide more guidance on how to identify the next right thing.

Anti-patterns

This is the appropriate place to discuss Sprint commitments. During Sprint Planning, the team plans the work for the upcoming Sprint. Old habits can creep into organizations doing Scrum as they focus on being *"on time"* – doing what the team said in the timeframe they committed to – as well as keeping to long-term plans.

Roadmaps are good, but hardened details can all too easily creep into those plans. Organizations marching to mid- and long-term plans likely are not iterating, meaning they are not learning from the experience of previous releases and adjusting. Rather, they act as *feature factories* knocking out what is next in the list.

To track how well the team is meeting its commitments, the organization pushes for more accurate estimates and tracks the team's *velocity* – the *"Agile way"* to track the amount of work the team accomplishes each Sprint. The team puts forth its Sprint commitment based on recent velocity as the expectation of what the team can complete in the next Sprint. Sprint burn-down tracking measures how well the team finishes what it said it would deliver. For some organizations, this becomes a *"success"* measure. More on success measures in Chapter Ten, but this focus on velocity is not represented in the Agile Manifesto.

Retrospectives

In Scrum, a Sprint Retrospective occurs after the Sprint Review following each Sprint. It is a time of reflection for the team to inspect how the previous Sprint went with regards to teamwork, processes, and tools. Whatever went well is lauded and set to continue, and opportunities for improvement are identified with plans to enact change over the next Sprint. Continuous improvement is the objective. *Inspect and adapt* in this sense refers to the team and how it operates.

A Retrospective is personal to the team. To be effective, team members need to feel safe to share, and have potentially difficult conversations. The goal is team growth and process improvement.

Agile Alignment

Retrospectives target the following from the Agile Manifesto:

- ❖ Manifesto Value: "Individuals and Interactions over Processes and Tools"

- ❖ Manifesto Principle: "At regular intervals, the team reflects on how to become more effective, then tunes and adjusts its behavior accordingly."

For teams not accustomed to continuous improvement activities, putting a routine in place to facilitate this type of discussion is helpful. When the scheduled retrospectives are no more than a month apart, there is ample opportunity to bring forth suggestions while they are still fresh on everyone's mind. The goal, however, is to address issues and opportunities whenever they present rather than waiting for a scheduled discussion.

Anti-patterns

Respondents of the Report cited Retrospectives as a key technique they employ, which is very much aligned with Agile. Interestingly, they also cited wanting standardized processes and felt a lack of them was one of the challenges to Agile adoption. The respondents seem conflicted.

Continuous improvement by definition should make standardization implausible. If each team is to inspect and adapt how it works, this should naturally create differences in how each team operates – it makes best practices a moving target. When standardization wins out across an organization, Retrospectives become meaningless or isolated to small adjustments – often adjustments that are pushed out across teams to maintain those standards.

Sprint / Iteration Review

A Sprint Review occurs at the end of a Scrum Sprint to inspect the product increment and adapt the backlog as needed based on feedback from the stakeholders. The team demonstrates to stakeholders what was accomplished during the Sprint, and what is ready to be deployed. Feedback should inform the backlog – create new backlog items, identify obsolete items, or modify existing backlog items. The objective is to support an empirical approach of do, experience, learn, and adjust. *Inspect and adapt*, in this sense, is for product improvement.

Agile Alignment

Sprint Reviews directly target all of the Agile Manifesto values. In summary, developers and the business collaborate by reviewing working software in order to determine the next right thing to do. According to the Manifesto principle "working software is the primary measure of progress," this show-and-tell ceremony allows users to see what was developed so that feedback can inform the next short iteration.

Anti-patterns

For the most part, the Sprint Review is a good process for teams working in Sprints. The reliance on the Sprint Review may potentially keep the team from bringing in key stakeholders to review work items sooner, but each team needs to decide who to engage and when. If there is not a problem to solve by having key stakeholders review and/or personally validate sooner, then this is a moot point.

Short Iterations

Short iterations come standard with Scrum Sprints or with the continuous flow of Kanban (story by story). This practice is very Agile and facilitates the opportunity for an empirical approach to both the product and the team's process.

Agile Alignment

Short iterations target the following from the Agile Manifesto:

❖ Manifesto Value: "Working Software over Comprehensive Documentation"

❖ Manifesto Principle: "Deliver working software frequently, from a couple of weeks to a couple of months, with a preference to the shorter timescale."

When teams use short iterations, the goal is to deliver something that works, something valuable, each iteration. With each deliverable, the opportunity exists to experience, learn, and adjust the product, and the process.

The reason I did not include alignment to the values for *individuals and interaction* or for *responding to change* is because a team can work in short iterations, or time boxes, while not necessarily responding to change or engaging each other well. It is a misnomer that teams doing Scrum are automatically Agile by working in iterations. Not true. To *iterate* is to learn and adjust. For many teams, *"iteration"* is synonymous with repetitive time boxes, such as Sprint, used merely to break up the delivery of a set of requirements.

Anti-patterns

Short iterations can simply become traditionally managed projects in smaller timeframes. Teams can fix scope up front and do whatever it takes to deliver the promises, and then measure success against how well it delivered the fixed scope within the fixed timeline. Short cycles, sure, but iteration, no.

Planning Poker / Team Estimation

Planning Poker®[11] is an estimation technique used by the team to come to an agreement on the size or effort of work. Although story points are not part of Scrum, many Scrum teams use story points to estimate the work in their backlog.

A story point is an arbitrary method, unique to a team, for sizing work relative to other work. The Fibonacci scale is a common numbering sequence used by teams to assign story points to each backlog item. The numbers 1, 2, 3, 5, 8, 13, and 21 are most common, where 1 is very small and 21 is extremely large. Each backlog item is given a number, or size, in relation to another.

Relative sizing may say one thing is three times bigger than another, but avoids specificity. This approach can be just as much, if not more, effective at estimating what a team can accomplish in a given time period than traditional hours breakdowns. I will discuss the merits of story points in more detail in Chapter Ten.

Planning Poker® is a process whereby each team member simultaneously flips over a card representing the number of story points they think an item is worth. This creates a conversation among the team until all agree on a size. The story points completed each Sprint becomes the team's velocity.

Agile Alignment

Neither Planning Poker®, nor any estimation method, specifically aligns with the values and principles of Agile. Consider the following Manifesto principles:

- ❖ "Our highest priority is to satisfy the customer through early and continuous delivery of valuable software."
- ❖ "Deliver working software frequently…"
- ❖ "Working software is the primary measure of progress."

What do these principles have in common? These principles focus on delivering something of value early and often. Why do teams estimate? I believe they estimate in order to track plans, schedules, and how well the team did delivering *"on time."* It all ties back to the need to know when and how long something will take to complete.

Anti-patterns

The whole point of estimating work is for planning work and timelines. It is nice to know how long work will take to complete, or how long it will take to burn through some set of ideas. The risk is focusing too much on timelines and measuring success against meeting those timelines. When success is all about being right with estimates, the team loses its freedom to discover, explore, and change directions as needed because that, after all, messes up schedules.

Kanban

It is interesting that Kanban is listed as a "technique" alongside Retrospectives and Sprint Reviews. Kanban is an approach to work that encompasses many techniques. At its core is the desire to visualize work, limit how much work is in progress at any given time, to improve workflow, and for continuous improvement. Most of the techniques in this list are Scrum techniques. Scrum can be purely followed as a self-contained set of practices. Kanban can also be purely followed as its own set of self-contained methods. This is why including Kanban as a "technique" alongside individual Scrum practices is interesting to me.

The reason it is included as a practice is because many times, as Scrum teams mature, they move away from some of the rigid time boxed practices in favor of more continuous flow approaches offered via Kanban. They seek to *fill the gaps*. Teams combine practices from both Scrum and Kanban – thus the term "ScrumBan." Some say this is a natural maturation process, likened to the Japanese stages of learning concept known as Shu-Ha-Ri. I will discuss this more in Chapter Six.

Agile Alignment

Kanban approaches align well with all the Agile values and principles. Kanban pushes individual items of work from beginning to end, with a focus on getting the work in progress done before pulling in new work. Unlike Scrum, where work is projected and committed to up front for the entire time box, Kanban simply pulls from the top of the list and continuously works based on the highest priorities. This pull method allows the team to always pull in the next right thing – assuming the team is prioritizing accordingly – and delivering potentially deployable work early and often. The goal with Kanban is to start and finish the most important work, as a team, before pulling in new work.

Anti-patterns

Kanban facilitates continuous delivery much better than Scrum, but still does not help with determining what should be done next. Yes, the team pulls from the top of this list, but determining what should be at the top of the list is still not something any operational framework helps with. Scrum actually provides a better opportunity to stop and reflect than Kanban. Therefore, the team can still get trapped into focusing on optimizing flow without optimizing value. The team can still fall into the trap of delivering planned scope, story by story versus via the batch commitments of Scrum. This is not really an anti-pattern as much as it is a separate issue to work in parallel.

Dedicated Customer / Product Owner

The Product Owner is one of the few named roles in Scrum and acts as the single business representative for the development team to engage with who prioritizes the work the team does. The Product Owner clarifies requirements, answers questions throughout development, interfaces with the business, validates delivery, and determines what should be deployed.

Agile Alignment

The Agile principle "business people and developers must work together daily throughout the project" is what Scrum targets with the single Product Owner concept. The Scrum Guide™[12] stresses a single owner to engage the development team, rather than a committee, in order to minimize the distractions on the team – for productivity's sake.

This single Product Owner concept is not Agile. Scrum isolates and shields the development team to increase productivity, but as Martin Fowler noted, everyone on the team needs to be able to engage with the business to be most effective. What you have to decide is this: is it better for the team to be able to work uninterrupted and get everything planned done, or to be able to interact with the business users and get the right things done?

Anti-patterns

What happens far too often is someone is named Product Owner that is not empowered, not knowledgeable enough in the product, or is not good at making accountable decisions. This creates bottlenecks. The Product Owner often is a designated liaison between the real product decision makers and the development team. This added layer injects delay, confusion, and ineffectiveness.

The other issue is that the Product Owner sometimes takes on project manager roles and directs the team more than Scrum intends, and certainly more than Agile intends.

Some suggest the Product Owner is not a needed role, that the team can make product decisions collaboratively. I see nothing wrong with a *Value Team* that discusses and provides input, but I believe someone still needs to be a final decision maker to resolve impasses and move things along.

Follow the Crowd Cautiously

"The majority is always wrong;
the minority is rarely right." – Henrik Ibsen

The bottom line is this, just because the majority of industry is doing something, does not mean it is the right or best way for your organization – it does not mean it aligns with Agile. Processes, practices, and tools need to undergo the same scrutiny as product features for understanding what problem you are trying to solve by employing them. Many solutions seem appropriate on the surface, but are you addressing the right problems and pursuing the right outcomes?

What I hope you have taken away from the book thus far is the need to always assess what you are doing against the baseline values and principles of what Agile really is and intends. Frameworks can be followed in an Agile way, they can also be followed in a not-so-Agile way. In the end, what you do is not as important as why you do it. Do your processes, practices, and tools support an empirical approach? Do they align with the Agile Manifesto? Does everything else you have layered on top of this foundation also align and support the true intention of Agile?

Chapter 6:
Agile is Not Agile

According to the VersionOne *12th Annual State of Agile Report* (the Report) released in 2018, 52% of respondents claim more than half of their teams are using Agile practices[13]. This is up from 40% the year before[14]. Agile transformation seems to be in full bloom. Not all that long ago, the challenge was convincing organizations that they needed to try Agile. Today, the question organizations ask is no longer "should we *do* Agile" but rather "how do we *scale* Agile?"

This is good news, right? Agile proponents have been pushing long and hard to get organizations to see the light when it comes to the Agile way of thinking and working. The "Certification Economy" is strong for there is no shortage of certifications you can pursue around Agile and associated frameworks. Everyone seems to be headed in the right direction...or are they?

"So that's our current battle...it's realizing that a lot of what people are doing and calling agile, just isn't."
– Martin Fowler, co-author, Agile Manifesto

I reuse this quote here because it is the crux of the matter – Agile is misunderstood and misapplied.

The previous two chapters exposed that what many organizations, even coaches, call Agile simply is not Agile. The Agile way of thinking and working is not necessarily what organizations are doing. Much of what organizations are doing, or not doing, is defined by traditional thinking and hardened cultures. This misalignment is leading to misapplication, although many organizations are not yet aware of being on the wrong path. Until these barriers are removed, nothing they *do* will help them find true Agile transformation, or organizational agility. Timeless Agility will remain out of reach.

Where the resistance used to be a pushback to the change itself, today the resistance is more about the drag slowing down progress as a result of misunderstanding and misapplication.

My goal for this chapter is to surface the root-level barriers to Agile transformation. In doing so, I will explore cause and effect scenarios that I believe got us to where we are today. Armed with a little historical perspective, my hope is that you will be able to better understand what is happening in your organization. The objective is to get you onto the right path, with the right thinking, to achieve what Agile always intended. How to do that is covered in the second half of this book. This transition into the latter half aims to arm you with a better understanding of what problem you have to solve, which is the first step to deciding on a path forward.

The Unintentional Intentional Distortion of Agile

Agile is misunderstood. The question I wrestle with – is Agile misunderstood because it has been distorted, or has Agile been distorted because it is misunderstood? There is no doubt that Agile has been distorted. What many organizations are doing, what is often taught, does not align with the intent of Agile. The question is, did this occur by accident or on purpose? I believe this is a case of unintentional intent to distort. Let me explain.

If you are in management or part of a leadership team, you know how hard it can be to propagate your values down into the organization. Despite having organizational rank and authority, it is still challenging to get everyone to embrace the same mindset and act accordingly. How much more so is the challenge to push a mindset change upward into and throughout the management team *without* the influence of rank and authority?

Respondents of the Report cited two challenges[15] that directly relates to this distortion issue.

- ❖ Organizational culture at odds with agile values
- ❖ Inadequate management support and sponsorship

What these responses tell me is that management may be in favor of their development teams *"doing agile,"* but lack the understanding that Agile transformation requires a mindset shift throughout the organization. Management *claims* successful Agile transformation while not embracing much of the intent of Agile. It becomes Agile on their terms.

It was (and is) typical for the desire to be Agile to first take root at the team level and then for those values and principles to be pushed upward into the management layer. This is why transformation can be so difficult. Many times that wall is too high to get over and culture remains the obstacle to genuine Agile transformation. A team may become more Agile in isolation, and within its own context, but that is not Agile transformation.

In order to proceed with this new way of working, early adopters conceded that they must still provide management with traditional output-focused metrics and accommodate traditional command and control style management. Despite being contrary to true Agile, teams compromised, feeling that something was better than nothing. This still happens today as well, but I am trying to give it a historical cause and effect context.

Management's lack of understanding and willingness to transform how work was done and measured opened the door for compromise. As more organizations became open to the idea of exploring Agile, training and certification companies provided offerings that straddled this compromise. So, in essence, the distortion was propagated intentionally in order to sell it and allow at least pieces of Agile to enter.

The "Certification Economy" grew while
true Agile suffered.

The organizations that brought in Agile practices on their own terms never really understood or embraced what Agile really intended to provide, so that misunderstanding propagated within their walls. Training and certification organizations accommodated this cultural compromise and their teaching reflected this distorted understanding. This is seen in the common metrics used to define *"success,"* which I will cover in detail in Chapter Ten.

Organizations wanting to learn Agile, perhaps with the right intent, were taught the wrong things – and still are today. They are taught that Agile thinking is for development and delivery teams only. They are taught that Agile is about being more productive and better at being on time. They are taught that using popular tools, writing user stories, working in Sprints, and having daily stand up meetings makes them Agile.

Coaching is now prevalent and accepted, yet what many coaches are teaching is faux Agile – ideas based on a misunderstanding rooted in the unintentional intentional distortion of Agile. This misunderstanding across industry has grown exponentially.

Many organizations do not even recognize this dilemma. This misunderstanding is sending organizations down the wrong path, or I can at least suggest that it is a less effective path. The downstream impacts of misunderstanding are cascading.

Increasing the productivity of every team seems to be the primary goal, so processes and practices that support more outputs are standardized and pushed to all teams. This is otherwise known as scaling. Yet none of that has anything to do with an empirical approach or the Agile Manifesto. Enter the *Streetlight Effect* and the *Hawthorne Effect*.

Streetlight Effect

A type of observational bias where people only look for whatever they are searching for by looking where it is easiest.

The Streetlight Effect[16] is a common phenomenon that suggests people will look for answers where it is easiest rather than where it is most effective or most telling. This occurs very frequently in how organizations measure success.

For example, measuring the number of lines of code produced is a real measure some organizations have used to gauge the productivity of their developers. It is something that is easy to measure, but does lines of code really inform you of anything? Consider two scenarios.

In one scenario, you tell your developer she needs to produce more lines of code because others are producing more. She responds, "Are you referring to the five lines of code that solved world peace?" Obviously this is an exaggerated example, but one that questions the value of the *number* of lines of code versus the value of the *outcome* it produces.

In another scenario, you are measuring your developers by number of lines of code produced, which is part of their performance appraisals. Your junior developers are writing 100 lines of code compared to your senior developers who are writing 50 lines of code to achieve the same results. Does 100 lines of code demonstrate more productivity, or effectiveness?

In an environment that focuses on lines of code produced, what might you expect to start happening? Developers are likely to meet management's expectations for more code by writing more code – the Hawthorn Effect.

Hawthorne Effect

A term referring to the tendency of some people to perform differently when they are participants in an experiment [or being observed].

When people are measured and judged by their productivity performance, something called the *Hawthorne Effect*[17] comes into play. The general notion is that when people know they are being observed and how they are measured, they will work toward desired results.

Team optimization is important, and this may seem like the right outcome, but as I alluded to in describing the

Streetlight Effect, is *more* really the measure of team success and will more give you the *outcomes* you should be pursuing?

From my experience, the other more likely possibility resulting from productivity measures is that people will game the system to make the observed data look better. Obviously the results become skewed either way. For example, you go to your team and tell them that they need to produce more story points each iteration – more productivity. Story points are a relative sizing technique that equates to the team's estimated effort to produce a thing. Teams focused on story points aim to optimize and deliver as many story points per iteration as possible. So, how can this team produce more story points? They can find ways to do more in less time, they can work more hours, or they can give bigger estimates.

Becoming more efficient is a valid Agile-aligned goal, but a team eventually reaches a point where they can optimize output no more. Working overtime violates an Agile principle around *sustainable pace*, so this is not a long-term productivity solution. Lastly, padding estimates meets the goal of showing more story points per iterations, but does not reveal reality.

Is more output what you really want? The answer should depend on what you are outputting. If you are outputting *the next right thing*, then yes, you want more of that. Otherwise, you may be outputting more of what holds little value to your users and stakeholders. A team can be very efficient at delivering new features, but if those features are not addressing the most impactful needs, does it matter that the team is doing more of what is not really needed?

What if instead of more output, the team desired more valuable output per iteration? How would that change how the team works and what it measures?

The team should absolutely work toward optimizing their flow. However, when their performance and definition of success is not tied to that, they are free to experiment and find that local optimization. When they are judged on it, they will usually find a way to meet the targets. That tends to produce measures that do not tell the truth, and therefore is not helpful.

The Certification Economy

I came up with the term the "Certification Economy" because professional certifications are big business. Organizations have always flocked to certifications, like the Project Management Professional (PMP)®, so a strong desire for certification as a Scrum Master, Developer, or Product Owner is no surprise.

Certifications do have their place. For one, the pursuit of a certification gets folks to attend the required training courses, which they otherwise might not have done. This can be a good thing, assuming the training is valuable and on point. Depending on what the certification is about, it can also demonstrate some baseline knowledge on a subject – at least the person passed the test. I believe the intentions of certification programs are good. The evolution of them, however, consistently brings unintended consequences.

Training and certification alone are not the issue. Where things went wrong was in believing that a certification means more than it does. The Certified ScrumMaster® (CSM®) certification from the Scrum Alliance, for example, is attained by sitting in on a two-day class and passing a test. The intent may have been to provide some foundational knowledge about Scrum, but it has been used by industry to put people directly into Scrum Master roles on teams – a role that requires far more skill and experience than a basic understanding of Scrum practices. The natural effect is that teams have floundered under these poor hiring and placement decisions. The value and power of that certification was (and is) misplaced.

I have spoken to many people certified in Scrum that do not know what an empirical approach is, despite it being referenced in the Scrum Guide™. Maybe I am being too harsh, but should not a follower of Scrum be well versed in the Scrum Guide™? Many have also never been taught the Agile Manifesto, or it has only briefly been presented to them.

As Chapter One detailed, Agile *is* the Agile Manifesto with a focus on supporting an empirical approach. These principles are why Agile exists in the first place. However, trainings quickly focused on what people should do and how to do it, as well as which tools to use. It became more about doing Agile than being Agile.

"The Agile that can be certified is not the true Agile."[18]
-- Andy Hunt, co-author, Agile Manifesto

It is much easier to build trainings and certifications around what you do versus what you think; or how you do something versus why. It is also the type of training organizations historically crave. Implementing and doing specific practices is tangible and scalable. This is what organizations wanted before Agile and it is what the "Certification Economy" offers them today. There is now some focus on training and certifying the Agile mindset, but the distortion and misunderstanding is a tall hill to climb.

The battle is doing Agile vs. being Agile. You can learn a new practice and tool in a classroom over two days, but transforming mindsets does not fit this model and takes time. I suppose the original idea was that certified practitioners would eventually help their teams and the organization expand its mindset, but cultural barriers keep the focus tight around its practices.

As the diagram below demonstrates, when an organization focuses on doing Agile, its mindset is wrapped around its processes and tools. *Doing* is following the popular framework rather than embracing a foundational value or principle. The *why* gets lost in the *what* and *how*.

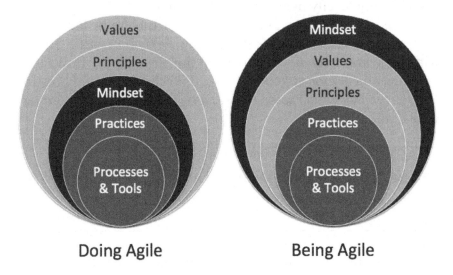

Doing Agile   Being Agile

When the mindset expands to envelope the values and principles, to allow those to dictate what the teams do, that is being Agile. Why you are doing something becomes more important than what and how. You are more willing to drop standards and best practices to do what works best for your team – aligned with those values and principles. You absolutely need to do things to work in Agile ways, but what problem are you trying to solve, what opportunity are you capturing, by following a specific process or using a certain tool? How are you aligned with the values and principles? How well does it support an empirical approach? When those are your first and driving questions, you are being Agile.

Misunderstanding Leads to Misapplication

When I ask folks to tell me what success looks like with Agile, the response is often around how well the team delivers the committed scope each Sprint – on time and on budget. When I ask how they know when a team or organization is Agile, the response is often that the teams are holding daily standup meetings, doing routine backlog grooming, Sprint Planning, Sprint Reviews, Retrospectives, and other Scrum-related activities. Many are not able to articulate the difference between Agile and Scrum. There is a widespread misunderstanding of what Agile really is.

As you seek Agile transformation, what is it exactly you are aiming to transform? Agile transformation is only as good as what Agile is to you. If your understanding is wrong, you will seek to transform the wrong things. If your understanding is incomplete, you will fall short on attaining all the intended benefits. Either way, organizational agility will remain out of reach, or incomplete at best.

In this section, I will explore a few common ways that misunderstanding is leading organizations to misapply Agile.

Believing Agile is Only For Development Teams

Agile trainings and certifications, particularly Scrum, focus primarily on how the software development teams operate, with a sprinkling of Product Owner training – the lone business representative that straddles development and business. Is that the right focus?

To create and maintain successful software products, your software teams need to be integrated with your business teams and the various product stakeholders. If only the development teams are living out the values and principles of Agile, there is going to be friction and misalignment across the stakeholder spectrum.

The common misunderstanding among organizational managers is that Agile is only something used by and done by teams of producers, such as software developers. Management completely misses the point that the lack of their own mindset transformation is a barrier to their organizational agility. This leads to misplaced expectations and puts the focus on the wrong success measures. Some of the bigger issues we ran to Agile to resolve remain in place. We are learning that merely changing the practices our development teams use is not helping to change our collective organizational mindsets. Culture is a barrier to success, and that culture is wrapped in the mindset that continues to go untouched by Agile values and principles because Agile is deemed only for developers.

Believing that Agile is only for software development teams is a hindrance to enterprise-wide Agile transformation

---

The "Certification Economy" plays a huge role in this problem as it is putting too much focus on how to do practices and processes focused almost entirely around the development and delivery team. What does this say to the non-development teams within your organization? What does it say to your organization's management? It says that they do not need to learn and understand what Agile is. It says that they can skip the trainings, they can skip the mindset transformations, and they can continue to expect the *same old same old* from their development teams. Development teams continue to be forced to compromise Agile's values and principles to meet hardened cultural norms, which were not effective before Agile and are much less so now.

Management will send their development teams to training, they will hire outside Agile coaches to come in and teach Scrum, and they will quickly look to how they can scale standardized practices across all the teams. It is common for management to be okay with their development teams trying this *Agile thing*, so their mindset seemingly recognizes Agile offers something they need. However, they still want their traditional productivity metrics and they still want enterprise standards for how Agile is done. Everyone beyond the development team needs to understand Agile equally as much and needs to participate in that mindset transformation. Otherwise, this disconnect creates a conflict that stifles organizational agility.

The Desire to Scale Agile

With a focus on frameworks and best practices comes the natural progression to standardize – to scale. Organizations love to standardize processes, practices, and tools, and the "Certification Economy" answered that call too. The Scaled Agile Framework® (SAFe®) and Scrum of Scrums are the two most popular approaches to scaling Agile today, but what are they scaling?

Scaling in this sense is about processes, tools, and practices. It is about spreading a common set of practices and tools across all teams and enforcing adherence. Organizations that focus on standardization strip teams' ability to optimize within their own contexts. Processes and tools become the solution and then everything else is built around those. This is the antithesis of Agile. How can each team follow the principle, "Build projects around motivated individuals. Give them the environment and support they need, and trust them to get the job done," by telling them how to work?

I am all for scaling Agile to achieve Agile transformation, but what is meant by *Agile*? Before you can transform your organization to Agile, before you can scale Agile, you have to know what Agile is and what transformation and scaling means in that context. We have already covered that Agile is the values and principles that support an empirical approach – it is not a prescribed set of practices. What these scaling methods are scaling is not Agile – they are scaling command and control structures. If that is what organizations want, then Agile is not the right fit for their purpose.

As I will discuss in more detail in Chapter Nine, scaling Agile should not be about spreading common practices and tools – it should be about propagating the Agile mindset. An Agile mindset enables teams to always be able to do the right things, effectively, regardless of the trends in practice or tools. When you scale the Agile mindset, you get closer to Timeless Agility.

Holding on to Traditional Measures

Traditional desires to measure output and to be *"on time"* have carried into organizations' Agile journeys. Much of what teams do is based on what they must report to management.

Organizational agility is not about how well you can keep a schedule, it is about how well you can identify and then do the next right thing.

When organizations believe Agile is about productivity, productivity is measured instead of value delivered. It is quite common that, despite using popular *"Agile metrics,"* organizations essentially continue to track to the same traditional measures as they did before – productivity and schedule adherence. It becomes more important to finish on time, or do what was committed to in the time committed to, than it is about learning and adjusting in order to deliver the *right* product.

The Shu-Ha-Ri Argument

Common wisdom suggests that we will learn to embody the values and principles of Agile as we do Agile practices – that we must first *do* Agile in order to become Agile. Shu-Ha-Ri is a Japanese stages-of-learning concept, often used in reference to the martial arts, and applied to Agile to describe how we progress in learning. The idea is that teams start off blindly following prescribed methods to learn the movements – the Shu stage. Eventually they learn the *why* behind those movements and make some slight adjustments to fit their unique needs – the Ha stage. Lastly, the team matures to the Ri stage where they no longer need prescribed frameworks to live out the values and principles they are following.

This Shu-Ha-Ri progression might lead your teams toward an Agile mindset, but teams more often than not get stuck in the Shu or Ha stages. Agile mindset proponents often inject Bruce Lee into the Shu-Ha-Ri conversation because his example supports where we ultimately want to go in our pursuit of Agile. If you are unfamiliar with Bruce Lee, he was arguably the best martial artist of his time, but his philosophy and the martial arts progression is what I want to highlight as it relates to Agile transformation.

Shu Stage

Shu is the stage where you are learning from a teacher how to perform something and you perform it exactly as instructed, in a very controlled manner, in order to learn the movements. If you liken this to martial arts, it is learning very static holds and situations in order to begin learning how to perform a move and to feel the resistance from your attacker.

When I practiced Aikido, I was told early on that moving out of the line of attack was the most important thing I could do, even if I never was able to perform a counter move. As a newbie, moving in such a way was not something I naturally did and thus I was not able to protect myself from attack because I was more focused on counter movements than simply avoiding attack. I learned to feel where energy and resistance is in static or slow movements so that I learned how to move out of the line of attack in a controlled manner.

In the case of Scrum, practitioners learn early on that one of the primary objectives is to work in smaller increments. They learn fairly simple practices such as user story splitting, Sprint Planning, Sprint Reviews, and Retrospectives. In the Shu stage, practitioners are not thinking too much about why or what the theories are beyond the art, they are merely learning how to perform the motions under ideal, or controlled, situations. This is exactly what it is like when Scrum is introduced to a team – they will do things aligned with Agile values and principles, perhaps without realizing it, but certainly will not yet *be* Agile.

Ha Stage

Ha is the stage where you are learning more about the whys and picking up on some theories such that you are able to make minor modifications to your movements, or practices, in order to adapt to non-textbook situations. Liken this to the martial arts where you go from static starting points to moving attacks that you learn to deal with.

Continuing with my Aikido example, this reminds me of a time when my sensei lined me up facing three attackers. It was a testing day for me, so I thought I would be dealing with each one individually, performing moves the sensei would tell me to demonstrate in a fairly slow-moving controlled situation. When he said, "go get him," I was immediately in a situation where I had to react to multiple attackers at once – something I had not yet done. This reminds me of the concept of "anything worth doing is worth doing poorly." I may have performed one or two moves well enough, but I mostly spent my time just staying out of the line of attack – not really having the opportunity to counter. My *what* and *why* were aligned with the ultimate objective, to protect myself, but my *how*, my execution of the movements, was all over the place. I was still following what I learned, but I had to figure out that some slight modifications were needed, no matter how poorly executed, to make it work now that the situation was a little more fluid.

Similarly in Scrum practice, something presents that is not *textbook*, or as learned in the classroom. The practitioner adjusts slightly while maintaining what they learned and within the framework. Working is smaller increments is a key objective. The practitioner is now able to evaluate the practices and modify as necessary to fit the team or situation. Perhaps the organization is throwing high-priority changes at the team rapidly. The practitioner realizes that meeting once a month for Sprint Planning is not effective to keep pace, so the frequency is moved to every other week for a shorter duration.

The Ha stage is also where you may be learning from other teachers, and picking up on some of those variations. You may understand Agile values and principles better now and use that understanding to modify your practices. For example, teams often find that incorporating some Kanban principles works best for the team.

Ri Stage

Ri is the stage where you now understand the values and principles of Agile well enough that you no longer are following specific teachers or practices exactly as taught. In fact, those named frameworks are limiting and constraining your team. In the Ri stage, you are fully capable of implementing your own practices, your own movements, to deal with your unique environment and situations. You may continue to use some practices learned earlier, modify others, but likely are doing things in a way that has no name of its own. It's a hybrid, if you will, or an altogether new way. But the key here is that everything you do in the Ri stage aligns perfectly with the underlying values and principles of Agile.

A team in the Ri stage is not following any specific framework or methodology. Existing methodologies could fade away and a team in the Ri stage would be just fine because everything they do will always align with the values and principles they embody. In other words, mindset transcends methodology for Timeless Agility.

The Bruce Lee Philosophy

Some suggest that Shu-Ha-Ri is like the belt system in Karate, mastering as you go. Thus, as you master Scrum, you move through Shu-Ha-Ri. Not true. Shu-Ha-Ri is not about mastering your art, or your framework; it is about *outgrowing* where you started and not being tied to any particular methodology for the sake of mastering one.

Ri is about taking the best from other styles and combining them with your own versions and creations to suit your unique situation. For example, Aikido combined Judo, Kendo, and JuJitsu. Bruce Lee created Jeet Kune Do having started with Wing Chun (a Kung Fu style) and was influenced by many fighting styles. Having something to model and learn from is not bad – not giving yourself the freedom to adapt and move beyond it is.

Bruce Lee, like us, started out learning a defined method. By doing something prescribed and controlled, he began to learn the mindset behind the art. But he eventually realized that he needed more flexibility, which only came from separating from structured forms and incorporating other forms into this practice. He focused foremost on what problems he needed to solve and created ways to solve them as efficiently as possible by borrowing, modifying, and creating his own practices. That is the Ri stage.

If the goal is Ri in your Agile transformation, and I hope that it is, you must develop your organization's mindset around Agile. This does not mean you will not be doing Agile-minded things. You will. In fact, the proponents of *doing Agile* will argue that people have to start doing in order to move past Shu into Ha and eventually Ri. The problem I am trying to address, however, is that organizations think that doing Scrum, or some other methodology, is the end all be all. As such, perfection in the methodology becomes the goal rather than adaptation. The focus starts with doing structured practices and never grows beyond that. This strict adherence mentality is keeping organizations from doing what actually matters, what actually works best for them. The reality is, Shu-Ha-Ri does not apply to Scrum, Kanban, or any other framework. It applies to Agile because the Ri stage is methodology independent.

I believe if you can focus your organization more on the why, more on the problem that needs solved, more on internalizing the values and principles of Agile, you can avoid the common pitfalls that are plaguing Agile transformation everywhere.

False Sense of Success

You are likely familiar with traditional waterfall projects. The name waterfall comes from the fact that all work flows sequentially in defined phases, where one phase must finish before the next begins. This generally means all requirements for the increment are defined up front, then developed, then tested, and then deployed. For many, breaking away from large up-front requirements documents and delivering software in two to four week increments makes them Agile. I believe this creates a false sense of success – a false sense of being Agile.

Despite common understanding, the issue is not so much the sequential nature of the work – all work flows sequentially, even single user stories. Even if you worked on and deployed each user story individually, you would still need to understand requirements before development; you would still need to test it after it was developed; and you would still deploy it after it was tested. Even a DevOps continuous integration and deployment process is sequential. Another misnomer is that waterfall's problem is its all-or-nothing focus, or what some may call big bang deployment. Again, even a daily deployment is technically "all or nothing" since the desire is to work on and deliver everything committed to for the increment. Rather, the real issue is batch size and frequency.

The problem with "waterfall" is not that it is sequential or that it is all-or-nothing – the problem is about batch size and frequency.

Breaking work into small batches (e.g. Sprints) and performing Scrum ceremonies does not make you Agile. Agile is ultimately about following an empirical approach where you do something, users experience it and provide feedback, you learn, and then adjust. The shorter those iterations, the more learning you have, the less risk you have, and the quicker you produce what users want and need.

Getting to shorter cycles requires more than just new practices for the development team – it requires rethinking how value is determined and who is involved in this process, and when. Cultures must change. The Agile Manifesto started the discussion around how teams can do things better and how the organization around them needs to support that different approach to work. The failure of traditional projects does not rest with development teams; it is an organizational issue.

Interlude:
What Problem Do You Want to Solve?

Your Problem Statement

Remember the problem statement I asked you to write down regarding what problem are you trying to solve by reading this book? It is time to review it.

Refer back to your original problem statement:

- ❖ Would you write it differently now?
- ❖ What would you change? Why?

Revise your problem statement, then seek ways to address that problem as you read the rest of the book.

"We can not solve our problems
with the same level of thinking
that created them"
-Albert Einstein

Section Two:
Addressing the Problem

"A journey of a thousand miles begins with one step."

-Lao Tzu

Chapter 7:
Understand Your Starting Point

Are you ready to pursue Timeless Agility and follow the path to lasting Agile transformation? In this chapter, I ask you to do a bit of self-assessment, both of yourself and of your organization. I recommend tackling transformation with a team, but even if you move forward alone, there are some skills needed for maximum effectiveness. I start with identifying what is needed from you and your transformation team. The bulk of the chapter helps you identify what to observe and take notice of within your organization. Knowing what you are starting with will help you establish an appropriate game plan.

"You can't change the world alone - you will need some
help - and to truly get from your starting point to your
destination takes friends, colleagues, the good will of
strangers and a strong coxswain to guide them."
– William H. McRaven

In full disclosure, Agile transformation is not easy, is not fast, and will not likely end up as you envision. Implementing new practices and tools is easy compared to aligning mindsets. Your organization may or may not be ready for genuine Agile transformation, but preparation begins with you. You are reading this book, so I know you are invested and serious about moving your organization forward.

I often say, "Anything worth doing is worth doing poorly," because getting started and making progress is better than waiting to figure it all out on paper first. Getting started in Agile transformation is no exception, however, the point of this book is to help ensure you avoid the *poorly* part of the process.

Your approach to transformation is perhaps the most important factor in the success your organization experiences. How you proceed from here is determined by where you currently are as an organization, as teams, and as individuals. The first thing to come to grips with is the fact that organizations, and most teams, do not become well-oiled Agile machines overnight. You should absolutely have a goal and a game plan for total transformation. However, *complete* enterprise transformation is rare. Like anything else, you will want to start where you can make those most impact.

The variations in factors that determine how well and how quickly your organization transforms its mindset are extensive. How open-minded is management, or the teams? Who has bought into Agile values and who is resistant, or merely unaware? Are your teams starting from zero exposure and experience with Agile, or do some team members have training and experience? Are your teams employing Agile methods today and are they focused more on *doing* Agile or *being* Agile? I could go on and on, but I hope you get the point.

An organization that is far down the wrong path is not necessarily harder to transform than one that is new to the concepts altogether. It is important that you assess the organization's current position and readiness for *real* Agile, and approach the transformation appropriately. Regardless, pushing forward poorly is still better than not going there at all, so let us get started.

Self-Assessment

My objective is to help you help your organization pursue Timeless Agility, so this section explores some of the skillsets you will need. Leading transformation is a major undertaking, so it is vital to objectively self-assess whether you are the right person for this job, or if you should seek some help. Seeking outside assistance is never a bad idea. I recommend you encourage a few others to read this book and work with you on this effort. Your transformation team should be able to cover each of the following roles.

Subject Matter Expert

Understanding the true meaning and intent of Agile is a prerequisite to pursuing Timeless Agility. Someone on your transformation team needs to embody Agile in its fullest. It is the lack of alignment with true Agile that sends organizations down the wrong path. Leading your teams from a position of misunderstanding will only perpetuate misapplication.

"Agile people gather into agile teams. If your people aren't agile, nothing else will be. Ever."
-- Andy Hunt, co-author, Agile Manifesto

Whether you band together with your colleagues to strengthen your Agile mindset or consider some one-on-one coaching/mentoring, the key for any transformation leader is to stay out ahead of where the rest of the organization is in the journey. This will help you better lead the group through its inevitable challenges. Always be a student of your craft!

Facilitator

Facilitation is the most basic function you will need to provide to any team. To facilitate, you need a solid understanding of Agile and how the practices the team employs align with Agile. A Scrum Master, for example, is first and foremost a facilitator of the Scrum practices. When they embody the true meaning and intent of Agile, they are better facilitators. When their Agile mindset is misaligned, the team suffers.

A facilitator needs to guide teams toward agreed-upon objectives and help them stay on the right path. A facilitator does not need to be able to know which path may be best for a team or how to initiate and affect change – that is where the *coach* and *change agent* roles factor in – but a facilitator understands what needs to be done to achieve the objective and how to guide teams in that direction.

Facilitation is sort of an art. The Certified ScrumMaster® requires only a two-day class and to pass a test. Many people are then put into Scrum Master roles, but the art of facilitation is often overlooked. Facilitation is about execution. Knowing what needs to be done is one thing. Knowing how to lead others toward willfully following and achieving the objective is another. Of all the skills listed in this section, facilitation is the one skill that carries over from traditional business activity.

Coach

Coaching is not a natural skill learned in corporate environments. It is an art and lifelong journey unto itself. Traditional business environments are command and control. This means that rising managers learn how to make decisions on behalf of others and then how to direct people to follow prescriptive processes and practices. Measuring and controlling how well individuals and teams follow those practices is how success is *traditionally* measured. Facilitation skills are learned along the way, but coaching takes on a much different perspective.

Some will say that a coach promoting Agile should never direct or tell teams what to do – that it is all about asking the right questions that lead others to their own success. I disagree with that, to an extent. A team new to Agile, or that is not experienced, does not know what they do not know. I believe the coach needs to guide such teams more directly than they would with experienced teams. This involves some instruction and advising. The team needs someone to point them in a direction, explain why, and then show them how to succeed.

Ideally, the coach works from the Ri stage in Shu-Ha-Ri and helps the team find the most appropriate practices and tools at every stage of their progression. In this case, no one methodology is prescribed and glommed onto. The coach helps the team pick and choose from a robust set of tools and practices that best meet their needs.

Can you advise your team on what, when, and how? Can you instruct, guide, and help them find their way? Sometimes the coach needs to make suggestions to help the team move forward. Other times the coach facilitates the team coming to their own conclusions while ensuring they stay aligned with core values, principles, and concepts. Are you ready to discern the difference and respond accordingly?

Change Agent

A change agent disrupts the status quo. They are not afraid to challenge cultural norms or management thinking. It should go without saying that they do so with tact and effectiveness. This is the most rare, yet influential, skill in your organization. There is no shortage of people with ideas for change, or those willing to speak up, but the ability to do so *effectively* throughout any level of the organization is special.

A change agent must be a subject matter expert in what they are seeking to change. They must be able to facilitate interest in fruitful discussion, and they must be able to educate and show why their recommended changes are worth pursuing. This person is comfortable talking with all levels of management about the organization's shortcomings and proposals for change – including cultural change.

The change agent lives and breathes continuous improvement. They recognize when and where change may help, what that change could be, and how to implement it. If a change agent *were* to lack in any of these areas, it would be more around implementation than the vision for necessary change itself. That is not uncommon, which is why the team needs strong coaching and facilitation capability to execute. A change agent that can bring all these skills is invaluable.

Mentor

Mentoring is perhaps one of the hardest skills to deliver. The Agile transformation journey inherently creates more facilitators, more coaches, and sometimes more change agents. If you are not producing more coaches and facilitators, your movement will not survive. As this occurs, teams and individuals mature in their Agile mindset and approach. What they need at this point is mentoring.

A mentor observes, asks questions, and provides insight. Where a coach actively works with you to affect change, a mentor walks along side you as you mature your mindset and come to your own conclusions. Mentors are sounding boards that can take you to the next level.

I say it is one of the hardest skills to deliver because it requires one to transition from actively leading to advising. You may start out telling the team what to do (Shu stage), and then help each person progress through Ha and into Ri, but eventually you work your way out of that job by replicating yourself and allowing the mature teams to go their own way.

Prepare Your Team

1. <u>Fill the roles</u> – build a transformation team with the necessary skill sets.

2. <u>Get on the same page</u> – read this book with your transformation team; align your objectives.

3. <u>Find a coach/mentor</u> – line up external coaching and mentoring to help you. *(see resources section)*

Pursuing Timeless Agility is a continuous process, and Agile transformation is a daunting task. Every step you take forward is better than where you are today, so the journey is well worth it. If you go into this with the right perspective and expectations, you will be just fine.

❖ There is no silver bullet – certifications, frameworks, and tools will not automatically make you Agile.

❖ You cannot simply hire consultants to "implement" Agile over the next *n* months.

❖ The process is very fluid so there is no one-size-fits-all solution to get you there.

I recommended in the Introduction at the beginning of this book that you go through this journey with others in your organization so that you can tag-team this effort. Hopefully you are doing that. If not, it is not too late to start building that team and getting on the same page. At this stage, I recommended you line up a mentor or coach that you can connect with as needed. This person will help *you* lead transformation.

Organizational Assessment

The *12th Annual State of Agile Report* suggests that most organizations have embraced Agile to some degree. I covered in earlier chapters that many of those organizations are looking to Agile for the wrong reasons, have the wrong understanding, and thus are not benefiting from the true intent of Agile. In this section, I will help you assess key areas within your organization that will give you some insight into your starting point. It may be beneficial for you to take notes as you go through this section. Some things you might specifically look for include:

- ❖ Desire to rally around an empirical approach

- ❖ Alignment with Agile values, principles, and concepts

- ❖ Divergence in alignment between upper management, middle management, and team members

Fit For Purpose

Since you are reading this book, I am going to make two assumptions. First, you believe that your organization can benefit from embracing the values, principles, and concepts defined in this book – that Agile is fit for purpose. Secondly, your organization is likely not working in complete alignment with the intended purpose of Agile, nor attaining its intended benefits. This creates a dilemma for you to reconcile. Your organization is doing what it is doing and has the culture it has because either the organization *rejects* the true meaning and intent of Agile, or it merely *misunderstands* how to apply it.

If the collective mindset and culture of your organization is what it truly wants and needs, then you may have to consider that Agile is not fit for purpose to meet the organization's objectives. Think about it, if the management culture is command and control, then Agile is not fit for purpose. If it is always imperative to deliver pre-planned work within pre-planned schedules and budgets, no matter what, then Agile is not fit for purpose. If standardizing processes, practices, and tools across all teams is engrained and desired, then Agile is not fit for purpose. Therefore, the only way you can move forward with Agile transformation is to believe that the actions you see are not what the organization really wants.

Before you embark on an Agile transformation, to change how the organization thinks and works, you must first understand what the organization is really trying to achieve by doing what it is doing. Does management really think people are not smart enough to accomplish organizational goals such that they need to standardize and tell people how to work and then micromanage that work? Maybe...but assuming that is not true, what is really behind these actions?

What if traditional command and control, and enforcing standards, was nothing more than blindly following what has always been taught? Traditional management teaching suggests that managers must decide what is best and then manage teams around that. What if managers believe that relinquishing that responsibility means that they are no longer needed, so they hold onto this approach out of fear?

Effective transformation starts with understanding and accepting the centrality of an empirical approach.

I find it very hard for anyone to refute the value of an empirical approach, *when they understand it*. Once that concept is bought into, you can work backwards to demonstrate how certain ways of working support empirical thinking, and how certain methods impede it. Using this concept as a baseline objective will help you identify alignment, or lack thereof, for anything the organization does. If the people within your organization cannot buy into the value of an empirical approach, then whatever you end up doing is not really aligned with Agile.

If an empirical approach is ever rejected as a viable method for your organization, then Agile is *not* fit for purpose. Therefore, you must first seek to understand how your organization receives working empirically, and then if the corresponding values, principles, and concepts resonate.

Take Notes

Action: Discuss empirical thinking with teams and managers across the organization.

Observation: How well is an empirical approach received; is it desired?

Action: If an empirical approach is well received, discuss the Timeless Concepts from Chapter Two. Optionally review the Agile Manifesto.

Observation: How well received are the Timeless Concepts and the Manifesto values and principles?

Who is Pushing Agile?

Where is the push for Agile coming from in your organization? Is management pushing your teams to adopt Agile or is Agile a grassroots effort initiated from within your development teams? One is not necessarily better or easier, but how you proceed will be influenced by who is pushing for Agile.

Regardless of where the movement originates, reception to Agile values and principles varies across the organization as well as its readiness for taking on what Agile transformation really entails. For example, a manager who initiates Agile may not truly understand the enterprise-wide implications of such a transformation and still ultimately can be a roadblock for success. Or you may succeed in selling management on the ideas behind Agile, but in the end it is the development teams that resist and hinder progress the most.

Management Push

Pushing Agile from the bottom up is very hard, so management pushing for Agile from the top down sounds like a blessing. Not necessarily. When management is pushing Agile for all the wrong reasons, that push tends to come with command and control standardization. Teams are forced to do Agile a certain way, ensuring that all traditional measures of success are adhered to. You end up with user stories and Sprints, and tools like Jira, but not necessarily an Agile culture.

A management push does not mean only management is pushing, or wanting, Agile. It merely means that management is active in the effort. With the right mindset, this is awesome. Without it, well...not so much.

Many managers learned that it is their job to come up with the *"best"* way to work, so processes, practices, and tools are decided and installed across the organization to support standardization. This is a product of traditional management education and organizational culture. If this is occurring in your organization, you have a management push. The challenge with a misaligned management push is, that to correct it, you will need to tactfully show them the *"error"* in their thinking and help them adjust while saving face.

Team Push

When you have only a team push, you do not yet have management pushing standards, which is good, but you also do not have support outside of the team to think and act in an Agile manner. Your teams may become progressively more Agile, ready to deploy software early and often, but the rest of the organization is not keeping pace with your way of working. This creates conflict and delays.

DevOps tends to be the natural next step for organizations once individual teams have been working with Agile practices. DevOps can facilitate the rapid deployment process that supports an empirical approach, but many organizations actually use DevOps as a way to standardize how work is done with a sole focus on more productivity.

If you do not have a supporting DevOps process, and there is not currently a plan to implement one, you are likely in a team-push only environment.

Take Notes

Observation: Are standards being pushed down into teams? Is there a supporting DevOps process? Is what the team is trying to do conflicting with management?

Why Does the Organization Want Agile?

Chapter Four spoke to the question of *why* organizations choose Agile. I noted that many organizations choose Agile for reasons not consistent with the true meaning and intent of Agile. Misunderstanding is the root cause of this misalignment. Understanding why your organization wants Agile is very revealing and will set you up for how to proceed.

The *why* will likely be different depending upon whom you ask. Management may want Agile because they believe it helps with productivity and predictability – to be *"on time."* Team members may want Agile because they do not have to document as much and believe they can work with less controls. Both perspectives are misaligned. If you are lucky, some will cite reasons that are perfectly aligned with the true meaning and intent of Agile. When you find those folks, recruit them for your transformation team.

Take Notes

<u>Action</u>: Ask a variety of team members and managers why they want Agile, what the benefits of Agile are.

<u>Observation</u>: How similar are the reasons given to the common reasons listed in Chapter Four; how do their benefits match the intended purposes given?

<u>Action</u>: Seek to understand why each person believes what he or she believes about Agile.

<u>Observation</u>: From where/what did the current beliefs come from?

Who is Agile For?

What is the collective organizational thinking around whom Agile is for? Is Agile for only the development teams? Is Agile only for the product teams? Is Agile something everyone in the organization must embrace?

The most common thinking is that Agile is only for the development teams – just look at Scrum adoption, for example. There is nothing wrong with development teams following Scrum, but Scrum is *only* for development teams. Regardless of methods chosen for day-to-day work, the values, principles, and concepts of Agile need to be embraced by the entire organization if true organizational agility is to be achieved.

Agile is an organizational mindset shift, not just some new practices a work team employs to output results. Is your management trained on Agile principles and methods? Is it a priority for your organization that everyone be formally trained in Agile principles? Agile transformation will happen faster and be more successful if the entire organization is committed to and actively pursues education and tangible experience employing these new concepts.

Take Notes

Observation: Are all business stakeholders engaged in the process or just a Product Owner or proxy representing the business? Is Agile training and coaching sought and provided beyond just the development team, and how far across the organization?

Agile Understanding

What is the overall understanding of Agile within the individual teams, across the product group, or across the enterprise? Let us explore management and teams, and consider a few points about each in your assessment.

Management

Managers are often taught and believe that it is their job to know what is best. To maintain that relevance that they fear losing, some managers may act like they know more about things than they really do. This goes far beyond just the subject of Agile, and it demonstrates a deeper cultural issue. This goes to the question of why do people feel the *"need"* to appear to know more than they do?

I talked with a manager once that was very confident in her understanding of Agile. She liked the idea of self-organizing teams so much that she told her teams to go figure it out. Without the help of a qualified coach or training, the team floundered and was berated for their lack of success. That type of manager is very dangerous to any organization, much less one trying to attain organizational agility.

An uncoachable manager is a non-starter.

Managers in this vein may have read a few books and articles and feel like they have it down. Broadly understanding concepts is not the same as having practical application and experience living them out. A manager who thinks he or she knows best, but really does not, is not very coachable and will be an obstacle to transformation success. What you may see in this situation is management contradicting and perhaps overriding what the coaches are trying to accomplish. This is like swimming upstream. The carryover effect is that the lack of humility regarding the lack of knowledge and experience leads to a lack of proper support for change. Without that, you will not be able to achieve Timeless Agility, and will struggle to find any agility at all.

On the other hand, I have seen managers operate in a very Agile-minded fashion despite not really knowing about or understanding Agile. The Agile way of thinking and working comes naturally to them and is just common sense.

How do you gauge your management's mindset around Agile? You observe - do they carry out in word and deed the values and principles of Agile? The further apart they are from living the values and principles, the harder transformation is going to be. That does not mean your managers are not going to be open-minded and willing to change. The key is, are they coachable?

Another thing to observe is how management solves problems. Do they invite the teams to collaborate and try things, or do they direct and put more structure and control around the situation? Are people and teams reorganized fairly frequently, or are teams empowered to leave titles and reporting structures at the door in order to find solutions and solve problems collaboratively? Any effort to fix problems with overbearing structure and plans is not aligned with Agile, so that would be another sign of where your starting point is.

For those managers that say they want Agile, do they expect some sort of Agile transformation project plan? Is there some type of thinking that says, "We will be Agile by x date?" Putting a plan and schedule around Agile transformation is treating it like something you can implement, like a tool or system. This thinking considers Agile as something to teach and mechanically do rather than something to become.

Are positions created for Agile Project Managers, or other similar Agile-titled jobs? This thinking also considers

Agile as something that is done, or a specific skill that one has. It is a common thought process – we *do* Agile, we get certified, and we stick Agile practices within legacy positions, like Project Manager. I chalk this up mostly to a lack of education and understanding, but it is still a sign that lets you know the current thinking in the organization – they are still thinking about doing rather than being Agile.

Is management still expecting the same reports and metrics from the project teams – GANTT charts, project schedules, earned value metrics, and percent compete? These are also clear indicators that more work needs to be done on educating what really matters and how to track it.

It is quite common for organizations to think they want to be Agile yet hold on to traditional ways of thinking and working. This is usually because management does not yet know how to report out on and answer to their bosses in ways that suffice. With time and experience, this concern will be resolved, if done right, so it is more about education and time than anything else. Know your starting point, know what concerns you need to help management address, and then plan around that. Management still needs to understand what they are spending and when to expect certain results. The value proposition is still important. Help management answer those questions within your Agile approaches and you will see transformation flourish and be supported.

Team

Within any organization, there are many distinct teams working on different projects and products. How those teams organize and then perform their work is greatly influenced by management and the culture of the organization. Teams in one organization may be under strict organizational process as directed by management and culture, which may not be based on Agile principles. These teams may appear to not be of the

Agile mindset, but that does not mean people in those teams are not Agile-minded and malleable to the Agile approach. On the flip side, teams across the organization may be flexible and less standardized in terms of what they do and how they do it. That does not necessarily mean management and culture support Agile approaches – it may just mean they are out of control. So, how do you assess your teams?

You observe - do folks carry out in word and deed the values and principles of Agile? Start by understanding, is your organization flexible in how its teams choose to work, or is it all about one-size-fits-all standards, or is it somewhere in between? How do teams and individuals react to their environment? If they are dictated how to work, do they talk about what it should be like? If they are given freedom to work as they wish, are they working by Agile values and principles?

Do your teams live out Agile values and principles, even if unconsciously? How do teams respond when presented with Agile concepts – are they receptive or dismissive?

Despite management's best intentions, teams have to buy into and develop Agile mindsets in order for Agile to work in the organization. Some people simply cannot work outside of strict routine and standards. They will have a hard time adjusting. On the other side of the spectrum, there are those who do not like any type of structure and control, and would rather just do whatever they want, however they want. That also will be a challenge to work through. Those folks will argue that they are already the embodiment of Agile, but in reality, they are missing the important point that Agile does not mean everything goes. There is still some structure and certainly accountability required.

Many of the same assessments given to management apply to individual team members. However, your team members are closer to the work and the day-to-day workflow. There may be varying opinions on how best to get work done and there are certainly different working styles across the teams. It is one thing to get management to agree on overarching approaches, it is another to get all the team members working together on common approaches. But for now, just take note of where teams and individuals are in their mindset and receptiveness to Agile principles.

One of the values of Agile is to work more closely and collaboratively with others versus relying on processes and tools to interact. Are your team members more apt to use email or get up and go talk with someone? Do they wait for scheduled meetings or address issues as they come up?

As much as empirical thinking can disrupt traditional management approaches, individuals can have an even harder time with moving forward with less information and pivoting quickly. I have worked with many developers that get upset when they have to redo something because someone's mind changed. It is seen as wasted time and effort that could have been avoided if more thorough analysis and requirements were done up front. Do you know anyone in your organization that thinks this way?

What about the other stakeholder groups? Do your users and benefactors of the product understand Agile and their role in the product management process?

Take Notes

Action: Talk with various managers, team members, and stakeholders about what Agile means and the benefits it provides. How do they believe the benefits are achieved?

Observation: Are the answers you hear aligned with the true meaning and intent of Agile as defined in this book? What are the differences?

Culture

Culture is really the totality of management and the teams that make up the organization. Management sets the tone. Teams react to that tone. The resulting behavior and attitude is the culture. I speak about culture separately, though, because culture can take on a personification of its own. The culture you see and experience may not really be the culture management wants and is striving for. Perhaps it is a work in progress. The culture is also not necessarily what the organization as a whole wants it to be – it just is, for a variety of reasons. How teams react to its managers and what they interpret from them varies and may not represent either what management wants or how the teams prefer to behave. There may be a disconnect, typically from a lack of communication.

One thing you can quickly see by observing is whether management prefers top down direct reporting structures or more flat and collaborative engagement. Certain businesses work best with top down direct reporting structures. This does not preclude them from being Agile. For most, I think the Agile mindset can and should be melded into the culture. If you are in an organization where team members are afraid or reluctant to step out on their own to make any decisions, if everything seems to require funneling through management, you are in a rigid management culture. Likewise, if managers feel the need to know more than they arguably really do, if they are afraid to give up control and decisions to teams, you have a cultural barrier to agility. Such a culture will be harder to break down and thus will require a much different approach for introducing and pushing Agile transformation.

Does your organization support a learning culture?

Perhaps tied to structured control is the attitude around trying new things and being okay with things not always working as planned; otherwise known as *learning*. Are teams punished for making mistakes or is experimenting encouraged? This is definitely a management cultural impact. Agility requires the freedom to explore and find new and better ways of doing work and building better products. Failure is embraced because that means the team is trying things and learning. A culture that does not support learning in this way cannot become Agile.

Is the organization facilitating and embracing change or is the culture one that makes a plan and sticks to it at all costs? Any organization that is not willing to walk away from its current activity to chase the next right thing, right now, is not working from an Agile mindset.

These are tones set by management and influence the behavior throughout the organization, which becomes its culture. Sometimes managers have the right vision, but need to adapt to the overwhelming mindset of its teams. Culture is not always representative of the management style – this is important to understand.

Are You Ready?

Transformation is difficult, which is why Agile coaching is flourishing, and why organizations still struggle to actually achieve the true intent of Agile. Circumstances across your organization can be complex, and every environment has its own unique challenges. How are you supposed to pull this off? Is there a system that provides an easy to follow step-by-step, fail-proof instruction for Agile transformation? Unfortunately, there is no specific checklist guaranteed to work every time, but there are some approaches I recommend, so keep reading.

Chapter 8:
Starting Smart

An empirical approach is about trying something, learning from it, and adjusting. The same holds true for Agile transformation. This is a journey – one that will take many turns. There is no such thing as an *implementation* of Agile, or an Agile *adoption*, or anything else that sounds all-inclusive and all at once. The key is to get started, but in a smart way.

You can't hurry the harvest by flooding the fields.

The previous chapter intended to help you assess your current landscape. Leading Agile transformation is a very fluid endeavor. How you proceed from here depends on the current landscape in your organization. If Agile is not even a consideration in your organization at this point, you have a much different road to travel than if the organization is already talking about doing something with Agile, and even more so if Agile has been practiced in some form for some period of time.

You will be working toward instilling a different mindset and getting your teams and managers to try new practices that support or reinforce that mindset. There is obviously a lot of work that goes along with that simple statement, so my recommended approach is to tackle change through *small bites* and *repetition*. I have never seen a successful large-scale change happen all at once. Similar to big bang, long-term software projects that rarely deploy as planned, if at all, transformation will not work that way either. Patience is required, picking the right battles at the right times is paramount, and continuously building upon your successes is the step-by-step process to pursue. If you come into this with the right perspective and expectations, your pursuit of Timeless Agility will yield fruit.

Understanding Team Dynamics

Understanding the dynamics you will see within teams will help you recognize the type of help each team will need in that moment. Not only will each team be in different stages at different times, but a single team can also fluctuate between stages. This point alone is good enough reason to allow each team to find their own way rather than being forced into enterprise-wide standards. How one team optimizes will, and should, vary from the next.

Tuckman's Stages of Group Development

Forming: Requires direction and leadership

Storming: Requires active coaching; conflict resolution

Norming: Requires light coaching and facilitation

Performing: Requires mentoring and light coaching

Bruce Tuckman first proposed the *forming, storming, norming, and performing* model of group development in 1965[19]. I introduce this briefly here to provide some basic understanding of how your teams will respond – to emphasize that this cycle of team development is normal and expected.

The *forming* stage is when the team initially comes together and begins to learn about its challenges and goals. Each team member is likely on his or her best behavior within the group as they are seeking to understand how they fit into the group and its purpose. It is more a group of individuals than a team at this point.

The *storming* stage is when the group begins to sort itself out and either gains some trust amongst each other or rifts form within the team. Opinions are voiced more freely now, which may create conflict and disagreement. Different working styles and personalities clash. Those who are inclined to lead are asserting themselves at this point. The duration of this stage can vary widely, and a group in the storming stage needs help to resolve differences and come together.

The *norming* stage is when the team settles in, builds greater intimacy, and a spirit of co-operation emerges. Individual goals make way for team goals and they learn to tolerate the idiosyncrasies within the group. Too much tolerance can lead to the other extreme where conflict goes unaddressed and unresolved. The team may appear to be working well but can stagnate and become the status quo.

The *performing* stage is when the team matures into an autonomous group that is capable of making most of its own decisions and resolving most of its own conflicts. Trust and safety emanates. This is the idea behind a *self-organizing team*.

A team can fluctuate across stages as they experience a shakeup in team leadership or team makeup. This is why it is so important to always have coaching nearby. Teams change over time and inevitably need help reaching the norming and performing stages again and again.

Take Small Bites

I learned a long time ago that to implement change, and particularly in government, successful transformation comes by way of small bites rather than large, sweeping changes. Just as an empirical approach works so well in product delivery, it works similarly for organizational change.

"Do not let what you cannot do interfere with what you can do." – John Wooden

---

I believe it is a mistake to attempt to *"implement"* Agile through some big universal push. Any large, sweeping change is going to be met with the most resistance. Trying to change everything all at once often leads to nothing being changed. If anything, the big ideas will be reduced to smaller steps anyway, so you might as well start there – it draws far less negative attention and resistance. If you do this right, you quickly progress through small, incremental changes that accomplish large, sweeping changes over time with much less resistance. The end result is better.

If the organization is open to making a big push toward Agile, it usually is treated as an *implementation*, which leads to standardization and trying to force a one-size-fits-all approach across all teams. The primary reason I believe this is a mistake is because Agile is then looked at as something you install and use rather than something you become and embody.

Processes and tools can be changed *"overnight,"* but mindsets take time to transform. You cannot work a detailed plan against a mindset change. When Agile is something you become, when it is the way you think, what you end up doing across your teams is not as important as the overall culture that is developed from that mindset transformation.

Furthermore, what you end up doing via the implementation approach will not have the effect you might expect if it is not also accompanied by a changed mindset.

The *small bites* approach is going to apply to both mindset changes as well as practices, and you will be working to enable change across both areas simultaneously. Regardless of what you tackle and when, my general recommendation is to focus on what is easiest to change first. I typically push for the highest value work first when talking about product development and priorities for what the team should be working on. Why then do I recommend the easiest over most impactful, or valuable, change when starting your Agile transformation?

When you are beginning the Agile transformation, no one understands the value-driven proposition yet and the highest value transformational targets may be the hardest and longest to implement. A series of small, quick wins builds momentum, and momentum is what you need in the beginning.

I mentioned before that the term "Agile" is distorted and misunderstood, but that I prefer to fight for its intended meaning and intent rather than run from the word. I am not backtracking on that, but I do think there is a time and place to use and not use certain words in the transformation process. It does not matter what the word or concept is, if words and semantics derail your message, then find less confrontational ways to describe the intent – for now.

Introduce small changes, make them work, and then introduce another. With success, trust builds, and people become more open to broader changes you introduce later. The meaning behind the names for ideas, concepts, and paradigms will always end up distorted, so running from them is not the answer. Correct the understanding of each term or concept after you help the team see it differently in action, but by all means, reintroduce proper names and references when it makes sense to do so.

Even mature teams continuously improve and change how they work. These changes are likely more practice and process related changes, since mature teams are by definition well established in their Agile values and principles. Change in a mature team still happens in small bites. Since the team is continuously seeking improvement, the change opportunities are small incidentally, so there is that caveat, but the point still applies. Small bites are best for all changes.

In the case of mindset changes, this is most raw in teams new to Agile through to moderately mature teams. Even teams with years of experience *doing* Agile may not be where they should be in their Agile mindset. You can send teams to training for a new practice or tool and they can likely come back and start using it. Changing one's mindset does not work that way. Mindsets change over time, through repetition of hearing, observing, and doing. "Seeing is believing."

Where to Start

Where you start, what your first bite is depends on many factors. I cannot advise what that is for you without being by your side. What I *can do* is offer some of my own experiences and how I came to decide my first bites.

I will highlight a few case studies I dealt with that may help you figure out how you might proceed within your organization. Each case study highlights the idea of taking small bites and focusing on the higher-impact, easier wins.

Case Study – "the next right thing"

The Situation:

- ❖ Contractor development team supporting many existing applications for various program offices
- ❖ Ability to deploy single changes to production at any time – little risk
- ❖ Long-time developers known well throughout the organization – fielding direct requests

Challenges:

- ❖ No organized change management process
- ❖ No visibility or accounting for the work done
- ❖ Time not spent on the most valuable work

Strategy: Focus the team on the value of the *next right thing* and to find ways to better manage priorities.

This case study highlights a common scenario in which there was a team of experienced developers that were set in their ways. They were not necessarily working by any organized standards and had been in the same positions within the organization for a long time. Everything seemed to be working fine, especially in their eyes, so how did I approach opportunities for continuous improvement?

I relish opportunities like this – to come into a fresh situation and find ways to help the team improve. I love the challenge. Every situation is unique – the culture, the people, the constraints, the problems they face, the team dynamics.

When I heard what the situation was like, I jumped at the opportunity to lead this team. I am certainly not unique or special, but I do think the person leading change on a team, or within the broader organization, needs this type of zeal for embracing all the facets of organizational change.

Several of the senior team members had been on the team and in the same roles for more than ten years. They knew the key program office personnel (the clients) very well, they knew everything about every applications they supported, and in their eyes they did not need a *boss*.

Teams that trust you will follow you anywhere.

Coming up through my career, I have seen new managers come into teams and start making changes right away. I knew that was not going to be effective. For one, I needed time to observe and identify what problem(s) needed solved. Change for the sake of change is never a good idea. Secondly, I needed to earn some trust in order to bring down the walls of natural resistance. Every team in existence can improve something, so it was without question that this team could improve in some way. My goal was to identify the most impactful change that I thought would have the least resistance, implement it, let the team see the results, allow that to build trust and confidence, and then introduce another.

I want to digress just a bit before moving on with this case study. I mentioned earlier that some professionals believe that coaches should never tell or direct people and teams. I also mentioned that I disagree with that notion because people do not know what they do not know. Sometimes they need a push. This case study is an example of that. The team was already doing what they wanted. They needed a push (or pull) to experience alternative ways of working.

Now back to the story. So I listened, and I observed. I met with each team member frequently to learn about what they do and the obstacles they face. I asked questions and contributed. I earned respect by offering some good technical suggestions. I helped them pick off a few of the obstacles they brought to me rather than pushing them to accommodate anything I wanted, yet. I coached and I advocated for them. Trust built. Then one day, when it felt right, I introduced what I thought was the next right thing for process improvement.

Before I get into what I went after first, let me provide some more background on this group and what they did. The team managed the routine support and enhancement for about forty applications. Each developer focused more on certain applications than others with one developer being the more versatile across the suite. The relationship each developer had with various program offices was such that the program folks went directly to the developer when they had issues or wanted something changed. The department had a ticketing system to track requests for support and changes, but most of these requests never made it into the system.

After observing for a month or so, I had two big concerns. One, I knew the team was busy doing great work, but the organization looked to the ticketing system to measure the volume of work and the type of requests being managed. Without having an accurate account for the work being done by my team, I feared that funding and the size of the team could be reduced. Some might say this was a management cultural issue that needed fixed rather than accommodated. Long term, sure, but I think we must work within our constraints to make progress.

The other thing that concerned me was that when someone from the program office showed up at a developer's desk, that request was what he or she immediately started working on. The concept of *the next right thing*, the next most valuable thing, was lost.

Despite the argument that it sometimes took just as long to log the request into the ticketing system as it did to just do the work, the team did not need much convincing that losing funding and people was a real risk as a result of their work not being tracked. Sure, you can argue that this approach was flawed, but I think you have to work within or around the constraints placed upon you. The team and the program offices also needed a way to *see* where their request fit on the priority list, and why. Logging the requests provided that.

The idea of not jumping right into the task brought by the program office was hard for the developers because they did not want to say "no" or appear to be unhelpful. That was understandable. With some proper communication, we worked through that with the team and the clients. No one wants their tasks pushed to the side in lieu of whomever just happens to show up at the developer's desk, so that was easy for the program offices to understand. I also provided cover for the developers by allowing them to put the blame squarely on me for requiring all requests to be entered into our backlog and prioritized accordingly.

This team was the poster child for the continuous flow of Kanban, but it just needed to make sure it was working on the next right thing and accounting for the work done. That, to me, was the first necessary change to enable. It really was painless and the team found that putting some order to the priority of work, and reducing their interruptions from the program office, improved their ability to get the most valuable work done. It was a positive change that continued to build trust. This opened the door for me to introduce more and bigger changes with less resistance.

This case study epitomizes the traditional software engineering lifecycle (SELC), which is heavy on documentation and process control. The program office and product team funded a development team from a separate contract managed beyond the control and influence of the program office. This is not uncommon within government, but it does two things. One, the program office has little control over how the development team works and the processes it must follow. Secondly, it puts the development team in between divided loyalties as it tries to meet the program's desires and adhere to their contract requirements. The program initially went along for the ride. This case study provides a glimpse into how change started.

I was on a contract team that supported the program office responsible for the product. The development team was a different contract managed outside of the program. It was initially an "us vs. them" relationship. How the development team worked, and the deliverables expected of it, was governed by an oversight body the program had no control over. The development team's true loyalty was to meeting the requirements of the contract, not how the program office wanted to work.

The program endured long and detailed requirements phases, long development cycles similar to going into a black hole, and three months of testing and process delay tacked onto the backend of the development phase. The process contributed to up to nine months in between deployments. My goal – to do what they said could not be done.

The program faced two barriers: one was the rigid contract, and the other was the adversarial relationship between the enterprise, the program office, and the development team. The enterprise chose a contract management approach that is not effective for software development. The program office grew increasingly frustrated with the required methods. The development team did not feel safe to change.

It was clear to me that any thought of drastic change towards Agile thinking and practice was out of the question. In this environment, assuming the sweeping change idea would not be shot down completely, it would have required an extensive effort to change. A team would have had to go off in traditional project fashion to formulate detailed requirements and design of the new process, and get signatures, before we even tried anything different. This would have required the contracting office and the development team to agree to a highly scrutinized and comprehensive process, which would have taken months, if it ever happened at all.

I knew from previous experience that successful change, especially in government environments, comes only in small bites. I understood that we needed to focus on fixing one thing, learn, and adjust – that defining everything up front was not realistic. I recognized that trust and safety was lacking and those thick walls needed to be broken down gradually if we were ever to bring the program office and development team together as one. Large-scale changes attract attention and receive scrutiny that easily kills initiatives before they begin. From experience I realized what we needed was small bites.

Two questions to consider:
What are your biggest problems right now?
Which of your problems seems easiest to solve?

I hoped that there would be some crossover of answers between the biggest problems and the easiest problems to solve. There was. One of the problems is that the program tried its best to think through everything it wanted in the requirements documentation phase. Once the program stakeholders saw the end product many months later, they found that it was not what they expected. That happened either because what they expected was misinterpreted, or most often, because they generally did not know what they wanted until they had a chance to see it and play with it. However, learning this in user acceptance testing, many months later, was the wrong time to learn that. The program needed to validate what it thought it wanted sooner and more often.

My first bite, my first recommendation, was to merely add a monthly review of what had been done so far. The sole purpose of this review was for the program office to make sure that what was being developed was indeed what they wanted and how they wanted it. No other changes were asked for at that time. Requirements would still be defined up front and in large documents. Work would be developed as the team always had. The program would continue to progress through the SELC gates. We assured the development team that these reviews were not about checking on progress or looking for defects. We simply wanted to validate the product stakeholders' requirements; catching mistakes would save everyone time, effort, and money. We stressed that it was to keep the program from going too far down the wrong paths.

This small change seemed harmless enough, it respected the contractual deliverables, and would close a big gap the team had. The product team would be able to see and validate that what was being developed matched what was in their own minds and expectations. If it did not match, or the team decided they wanted something different, they would have an open door to correct course before it was too late. However...this recommendation was still met with resistance. Resistance was not because anyone thought it was a bad idea; resistance was a result of not feeling safe.

Customer collaboration over contract negotiation

Under this development contract, a complete business and functional requirements document needed to be finalized and signed before any design and then development work could begin. The development team would go off for six months or more developing and thoroughly testing the work before holding an "official" review gate where it would be turned over for user acceptance testing (UAT). Contractually, the development team was *"dinged"* for any defects or missed requirements found in UAT. When the program office thought they were getting one thing and ended up with another, despite what the requirements document said, the situation was contentious. As a result, the development team refused to allow the program office to see anything until it had been thoroughly tested and validated on their end. The contract supported that decision, and the decision was driven by fear and a history demonstrating a lack of trust.

Given that background, imagine how the development team felt about the idea of showing work in progress to the program office. We had to assure and reassure the team that it was ok to have some issues – that this was the point of early review. Agreement to proceed with this small change took many discussions and took time and experience to gain some trust – that the program was trying to collaborate as *one team* to get it right rather than treat them as *"hired help"* working against factory specifications.

We used the term "Sprints" to identify these month-long development cycles that were between reviews. We used the term "Sprint Review" to name the review checkpoint. Rather than the development team doing a demo, several members of the product team logged in to see for themselves. Again, this was not about what the development team delivered, as a status, but rather was the product headed in the direction the program envisioned.

The natural desire you will wrestle with is to want to fix everything all at once. There are so many areas for improvement, from better defining value, to focusing on the most important things first, improving team collaboration, delivering more frequently, building a safe environment to experiment, and so on. We can debate why I started where I did in this case study, and why I chose the next steps I did. Maybe I would do it differently given the chance, maybe not. In the end, we got started and the team has continuously changed and improved ever since. Remember, transformation is a journey that starts with the first step, or bite.

For more insight into this case study, the next bite we took was introducing the concept of user stories instead of detailed business requirements. Since it was already obvious that defining details up front was not ideal, this change took the teams to the next level of learning to be more comfortable with not knowing every detail before starting to build something. The product team learned to first define the problem to solve, then the business need, and gradually let go of control of details to trust the developers to figure out how best to deliver the solution to their defined problems. Team balance and trust began to improve.

Then the team moved from defining an entire six months of requirements to defining them month-by-month, but with the same release duration and process. We called this "Sprint Planning." Now the team was learning that it did not need to define requirements too far in advance because they learned that this practice was wasteful since many of those requirements would become less important or change months later. In their business, needs change rapidly, so looking only one to two months ahead with any specificity was the most appropriate.

Move away from thinking about "implementing" Agile. Rather, think about the problems you want to solve and then find Agile ways to change. Inspect and adapt.

We took small bite after small bite. We sought the easier wins and took what was available to take. Each change was met with some resistance, more so early on than as trust was gained. As one change began to get comfortable, we introduced another. It is an ongoing journey, but how the team works today is night and day from where it was.

Some might look at the slow and steady approach we took and wonder why we did it this way. Why not change more, faster? Nine months to deploy!? Why not tackle that problem first? The challenge we always faced, and the dilemma the development team was caught in, was that they wanted to work with the program office, but needed to appease the contract. Figuring out how to do that and learning how to feel safe within such an adversarial contract was no small ask.

We were pushing Agile thinking and practices from the bottom up, bite by bite. We needed to recognize what the teams and the enterprise could accept, and when. To use a baseball analogy, you have to take what the pitcher gives you. If the pitcher is hitting his spots low and away, you will not have an opportunity to hit the homerun, unless he makes a mistake and lays one over the plate. Rather, you take what is given and do your best to move the runners over. When you try to do too much, you end up making outs.

Timing is everything. Pick your battles wisely.

Ultimately, creative solutions from smart people found ways to work together in more Agile ways while still providing the oversight body the contractual deliverables they wanted. That was our approach. Yes, it was compromise, but always with the intent of continuously pushing for change. What you tackle and when will vary on your circumstances. There is no one-size-fits-all approach and no step-by-step sequence that I can publish and you follow. This is just an example of how I assessed this one particular situation, found ways to keep moving forward, and got the team and organization closer to becoming Agile. I do know that trying to change everything all at once – trying to hit the *"ideal"* right away – is rarely effective.

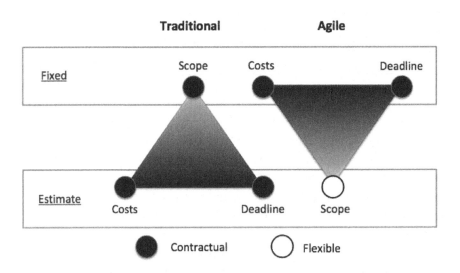

Case Study – "timeline in our favor"

The Situation:

❖ Development contractor team with a fixed budget and fixed timeline (1 year)

Challenges:

❖ Needed initial capabilities within two months

❖ Program details and requirements evolving

❖ Limited time and budget

Traditional   **Agile**

Fixed   Scope   Costs   Deadline

Estimate   Costs   Deadline   Scope

⬤ Contractual   ○ Flexible

I touched on this project in Chapter Two as an example for taking a *value-driven* approach to your work. I use it again here because this case study is the perfect example of why Agile approaches are ideal for most organizations. You may have seen something similar to the graphic above that indicates Agile projects have fixed time and budget, but scope needs to be flexible – the team delivers as much as it can within the time and cost allotted. Conversely, most projects start with a fixed budget, define a fixed set of scope, and set a target timeline, or schedule. Traditional project management starts off at a disadvantage because the money is fixed, the schedule is often arbitrary, and the desired scope is rarely realistic for both the time and money allocated. Invariably, experience tells us that rarely do all three remain fixed unless quality is reduced. This is the age-old dilemma that begs the question, why try to lock in all three for the sake of saying the team guessed right up front?

In that graphic, fixing time and cost is fine, so long as you are flexible with what gets delivered for that time and cost. This is hard from a traditional mindset because the business often does not trust the development teams will work hard without being pushed against those traditional constraints. What the graphic does not show is that scope *could* be fixed (although not empirical), but then time and money should be flexible. This case study provided fixed time and cost, so I used it to teach the organization about the flexible scope approach.

I was the contractor program lead for the development team working from within the technology department of a government agency. Our team provided software development to the program offices. The agency, nor the teams, had ever *knowingly* worked in an Agile way before. It was a traditional waterfall-style environment, though much less rigid than my previous case study. The program office created a work order allocating a fixed budget over a one-year period to develop a new case management application. This application would be used to support a new program they were launching to help ex-felons receive job training, assistance getting jobs, and then to follow up and track their process in the program. For the program to justify continuing, it not only had to help ex-felons obtain employment, but retain employment status.

One challenge we faced was that applicant intake would begin in about two months, and the program office had not yet defined all their requirements for their program, much less the application. For a traditional project environment where all requirements needed to be defined and signed off on prior to beginning work, not knowing all those requirements presented quite a problem. Additionally, even if the requirements were known, there was no way to get through requirements, design, and development of an entire application within two month so that applicant intake could begin. The situation served me the *iterative and incremental* approach on a silver platter.

First make it work; then make it work better.

Delivering minimum capabilities before time and money ran out was priority number one.

The only way we were going to be successful was to deliver what the program needed at the time it needed it, and focus entirely on minimum viable product (MVP). The first thing I did was to understand the progression of applicants through the program, and when those first applicants would progress through each stage. For example, applicant intake would begin in two months, so we knew that some basic applicant intake module was needed at that time. Tracking training provided to applicants would begin shortly after that, so that was our next module. Another month or so would need to pass before the applicant was ready for job assistance, and then follow up would be needed once jobs were given. Reporting capabilities would be needed last.

This project presented the perfect opportunity to help the business understand the need for thinking minimum capability to start. The approach I recommended was to deliver the bare minimum capabilities and user interface needed for each module, or step in the program. Our goal was to deliver the MVP for each module *just in time* for the case managers to use it in the applicant's progression. This was the first priority.

Since the program office had not fully fleshed out its own program requirements, we knew that they would learn more about what they needed once they started working with applicants and using the application. We further suggested that *required* changes for previously deployed modules could be implement along the way as well, but to keep those to only what was truly necessary.

I knew that there would at least be some additional annual funding to maintain the application after this project. Ongoing enhancements could be taken care of through that support contract. What I could not allow to happen is to run out of project funds without at least all the basic ability to manage the entire program's case management.

What I hope this case study does is help you see how you can use the very common situation where funds are allocated and timelines are envisioned, but where you can ease your business into holding more loosely to *expected* scope. Perhaps you work where the developers are on staff, or on a fixed contract like this case study. They are paid to be there every day, so you know their cost – that is fixed.

Next is to determine if there are any *real* deadlines to work with. In this case study, there were real deadlines to keep up with. Real deadlines require the organization to think seriously about what is necessary and what is not – MVP. There was fixed scope, to some degree, as the program needed specific modules for specific purposes. What were not fixed were the details. An empirical approach and MVP is the key to flexible scope while you work within fixed time and cost.

Chapter 9:
Scaling Agile

Scaling Agile in pursuit of Timeless Agility is about propagating the Agile mindset, which enables teams to always be able to do the right things, more effectively. In this chapter, I will provide some practical advice for how to scale Agile thinking across your organization.

Scaling mindsets may run contrary to how you think about scaling anything. When you scale your computing capacity, you spin up replicated environments that look the same, work the same, and provide the same expected performance. When you scale up a call center, you add more people to an existing process, using the same tools, and following the same scripts. To many people, it makes perfect sense why scaling Agile means inserting standardized processes and tools into teams. The assumption is that processes, practices, and tools are plug and play for any team.

Traditional scaling approaches do not apply to software product development because software is knowledge work that relies on an empirical way of working. It is more about the people than the processes and tools they use. Processes and tools do not make teams Agile – how they think, and approach work does. This usually requires *mindset* transformation, which takes time. Scaling Agile, therefore, is a matter of propagating the Agile mindset throughout the organization.

Establish Your Transformation Team

Similar to traditional scaling approaches, the source from which all else are replicated needs to be well established. Will that source be you, someone else in your organization, or someone you bring in to assist? Do you have a team of people in mind that will emanate the Agile mindset? This team will need to be firmly rooted in Agile values, principles, and concepts if the true meaning and intent of Agile is to be circulated throughout your organization.

> The transformation team helps scale Agile
> and as a byproduct scales itself.

Size of the Transformation Team

You might think the larger the team, the better, but not necessarily. A larger team can reach out more, and theoretically scale faster, but that presumes the proper mindset exists across the larger team. This is something you will need to assess since you have insight into how your colleagues think and how they receive the concepts laid out in this book. It is more important to have alignment than numbers.

I recommend starting with fewer people until you feel more comfortable growing your transformation team. Scaling your team is part of this process. As individuals within the organization transform how they think to align with Agile concepts, you will inevitably find new candidates for the transformation team. Each person on this team must be able to carry forward the unified mindset you are trying to scale.

You might be wondering, am I suggesting that you cut out any alternative viewpoints and ideas from the team around how to be Agile? What about self-organizing teams figuring out how they want to work and sharing ideas?

When it comes to defining Agile values, principles, and concepts, there cannot be alternative viewpoints. These are the *whys* behind what you do and how. That *why* is often misunderstood and distorted. Timeless Agility requires aligning with the true meaning and intent of Agile. You want, and need, a team unified around that. *How* work is done around that alignment *is* open for teams to explore.

Are teams supposed to be self-organizing? Ideally, teams reach that point, but only after they learn to embody the true meaning and intent of Agile. Otherwise, they will be organizing around distorted understanding – the problem we are trying to solve. Coaching is designed to help those teams get there and to no longer need *active* coaching – the transition into mentorship. You want teams engaged in defining their way, but a coach who is aligned with Agile aids that transition.

Can you identify one or more people that you believe are already aligned with Agile as defined in this book? Can you identify anyone that might understand true Agile if given the opportunity? Have them read this book and see how they align on these ideas. You are looking for alignment. The last thing you want is for competing and conflicting messages coming out from different people on your transformation team. Your organization needs to experience the same mindset from everyone on your transformation team. If that means you start alone, then start alone. Ideally, you will find at least one or two others to move forward with. If you are blessed and have more, awesome, just make sure you are all on the same page.

Filling the Roles

In the *self-assessment* section of Chapter Seven, I noted various roles that are required to lead Agile transformation:

- ❖ Subject Matter Expert (SME)
- ❖ Facilitator
- ❖ Coach
- ❖ Change Agent
- ❖ Mentor

These are the *roles* you need on your transformation team. These are not five separate people – one person could fill all five roles. Not every member needs to be able to fill every role, but every member needs to fill at least one role and be used *appropriately*. Naturally, the more roles one person can fill, the better. I would avoid single-role fillers unless you absolutely need that person to satisfy an unfilled gap.

At a minimum, everyone on this transformation team needs to believe and understand the values, principles, and concepts defined in this book if they are to help others adopt this mindset. They should be Agile SMEs. Everyone may not live them out perfectly – meaning the desire is there but they are still maturing – but each person must agree with the true meaning and intent of Agile.

The mistake some organizations make is putting people into these roles when they do not align. If your organization has already made that mistake, you now have the opportunity to counter that by forming this transformation team. If your organization seems to be pointed in the right direction, then use this opportunity to put some purpose and intentionality behind your transformation. Scaling the Agile mindset, replicating this way of thinking and working, starts with an aligned transformation team.

Community of Interest

Teams fortunate enough to have access to a coach benefit from that exposure. What about the teams that do not have interaction with a coach? What about management teams and the non-development teams that need to understand Agile thinking and how that plays into organizational agility? Enter the Community of Interest (CoI).

A CoI is a group of people that want to learn about a common topic, such as Agile or Timeless Agility, and come together to discuss and learn about the topic. A CoI does not require any prerequisite experience or proficiency. For contrast, a Community of Practice (CoP) is a group of specific practitioners (e.g. Scrum Masters, Product Managers, Testers) that share practices and experiences with other "experts" in their tactical area of work.

The topic of Agile or Timeless Agility is not specific to a type of practitioner – it is of interest to all – so a CoI is ideal for the entire enterprise to join and learn. It may seem like semantics to choose CoI over CoP, but optics matter. A CoP focuses on best practices that are about *how* to best do work in a given practical area. "Mindset Transcends Methodology™" is not just a catchy slogan; it is the premise of Timeless Agility. When your focus is on transforming mindsets, you want to stay clear of any indication that the group is about best practices.

This is not to say that you will not find legitimate opportunities to spin up one or more Communities of Practice. Your coaching team or Product Managers could certainly create their own CoP to more formalize the gathering and learning among that specific focus area, but for the broader organization, the Community of Interest is likely the best fit right now.

Who Belongs in a Community of Interest?

Everyone in your organization belongs in your Community of Interest. You might call it your Agile Community of Interest, but since many think Agile is only for development teams, that name might also make many people feel like it is not for them. Perhaps the Pursuing Timeless Agility Community of Interest is more inclusive. Maybe the entire organization can get behind the "doing the right things, more effectively" mantra. One merely needs to be interested in the topic to be a candidate for this group. Your CoI and your Agile transformation will be far more effective if you can touch minds across the enterprise. They all belong and will benefit – you now have to figure out how to get them there.

When a CoI Already Exists

What if your organization already has a Community of Interest or something similar? My answer depends on what is already in place and what your level of influence and reach is in your organization.

- ❖ Is there a clear gap between what is provided and what you know is needed?
- ❖ At what level is the community – is it within a small division, a larger department, or enterprise-wide?
- ❖ Is a new CoI needed or should you try to get more involved in the existing one(s)?

Is your area of the business well represented in the existing CoI? If not, it may make sense to create a CoI that better includes and relates to your part of the organization. I would use what is already available, if possible. Can you get on the existing presentation schedule? Can you find ways to engage the existing discussions? Use these opportunities to stimulate discussion and questions around existing thinking. Either you can position yourself in a more influential manner or you can identify others you can collaborate with to properly organize a *true* Agile transformation.

The Community of Interest Kick-Off

Starting and growing a community is hard work. It can take a while to build your audience to the point of it being fruitful. Even within an organization where managers strongly encourage participation, attendance can still wane over time.

What I find frustrating is that every meeting intends to share great content that *everyone* needs to hear, but rarely is everyone that can benefit from the discussion present at any one meeting. In a CoI, your coaches will likely present some information to the group and attempt to engage them on the topic. A good bit of effort will be put into preparation. Your transformation team may have a progression plan in mind for this material, so when attendance is low, it can be frustrating.

Gain Approval

Why would management agree to allow you and others to spend time on a Community of Interest? After all, you are asking for many people to spend time away from *"normal"* business activity to attend a thirty to sixty minute gathering once or twice a month. What you end up with will be impacted by whether or not your business is a *learning organization*.

---

*Learning benefits the organization just as much,
if not more so, as knocking out tasks.*

Some managers think *learning* needs to happen *on your own time*. That compromise is where "lunch and learns" comes from. This thinking originates from productivity-minded organizations that believe people should be solely focused on doing work tasks while *"on the clock."* Agile-minded organizations understand that learning and continuous improvement happens *on the job*. Learning is every bit as important as anything else that can be done.

Doing trainings over lunch does not place value on the learning, and attendance suffers. "Lunch and learns" say *optional*. Rather, schedule your CoI meetings and other short training sessions during the day and send your people to them.

If you must do the CoI meetings over lunch, so be it, just make sure to sell the idea and get it started. Consider, at this point, that what your approver thinks Agile is may not align with what you know it to be, so just focus on selling the broad idea of a CoI before getting into correcting any mindsets.

Benefits for Approving a CoI

❖ Aligning the approach for organizational agility
❖ Learning how to do the right things, effectively
❖ Continuous learning and improvement

The three bullets above are vague enough to avoid getting trapped in bad terminology or preconceived notions. How can anyone say "no" to alignment of approach, doing the right things more effectively, or continuous improvement?

Gain Interest

You might be able to gain approval and then proceed with gaining interest. Otherwise, you might need to gain interest before gaining approval. Whether you do this step first or second depends on your situation. Ultimately, you will need to answer the question, why would anyone want to join the Community of Interest?

One of the most effective tactics is to talk with people about the idea and the benefits. Face-to-face enthusiasm is extremely infectious. Call it salesmanship if you want, but all good ideas are sold, even if money never changes hands. You want interest to build so that you can start with a healthy-sized audience. Building grassroots interest is also a way to ensure you get approval from your decision makers. If many people want it, it will more likely get approval.

You may not know everyone in every team, so for that, talk with their managers and encourage them to encourage their people to attend. What you are doing initially is rounding up a startup audience for your kick-off series.

Kicking Off the Community of Interest

You have approval to proceed and have generated some interest. The next step is holding your first meeting. When you hear the term "kick-off," does that initially imply a single, first meeting that sets the stage for what is to come? I propose that your kick-off be slightly different. Rather than a single kick-off meeting, I recommend you split it into three separate meetings.

> ## Benefits of a Three-Part Kick-Off
>
> ❖ Reaches more people
>
> ❖ More emphasis on key points
>
> ❖ More input from members

When you hold a single kick-off, obviously only those in attendance hear the message. Word spreads about your new CoI and the meeting is forwarded to others – new people join each successive meeting. This pattern continues in the early stages of the group. You will invariably have some new members each meeting, at least for a while. The three-part kick-off attempts to accommodate that early growth pattern.

Whatever you would put together for a single kick-off simply split that into three parts. On the second meeting, do a quick review of what was covered last time and then add the new content. On the third meeting, do a quick review of parts one and two and then finish with part three. Any new members you get for the second and then third meetings will be exposed to all your kick-off content. This reaches more people, it helps you emphasize key points each time, and the input and engagement you have regarding the CoI concept increases.

Leading the CoI Meetings

Someone has to lead or facilitate the Community of Interest, for logistics' sake. That facilitation comes from your coaching team. In the early stages of your transformation initiative, I think you need more education pushed than open discussion. There is no one right way to do this, but here are some ideas.

Cadence

Having a meeting cadence is crucial. Schedule something recurring at least once a month, perhaps every two weeks if you can support it. The same day and time helps members clear their calendars and get into a routine.

Agendas

You want each CoI member to show up every meeting and take in whatever topics come up that day, but that is not reality. An agenda is common courtesy to inform your members about what will be covered in the meeting. It may help them decide to skip today, or it may help them decide to clear out any other competing priorities because they need to learn today's topic.

Plan out your agendas as far in advance as possible so that members can see what topics are coming and plan accordingly. These topics can be brief presentations or facilitated discussions. Perhaps consider doing one of those planned topics every other meeting and then in between doing a *coaches corner*, or something similar. With this format, the group has the opportunity to ask questions and engage on many smaller topics throughout the discussion.

Start On Time

Whatever your start time, start when it is that time. This shows respect to those that showed up on time and hopefully gets the point across to stragglers that punctuality is important. Showing up late interrupts, and latecomers miss whatever happened prior to them showing up. Resist the urge to go back and recap for those that show up late.

There are two primary reasons why people show up a few minutes late to your meetings – either they are simply not good at being punctual, or they are coming from a back-to-back meeting. When your start time is exactly their last meeting's end time, you will have latecomers to your meeting. When you start your meeting on time, your first five minutes or so will be constantly interrupted by late call-ins and show-ups. Half the group misses your attention-grabbing introduction.

You can reduce this impact by setting your meeting start time at 5-10 minutes after the hour. This will not resolve the issue of late joins by those who tend to just be late, but it will help get those in back-to-back meetings an opportunity to join and not miss out.

Engage the Audience

No one wants to sit and listen to a long presentation without any engagement. You will see people in the room nodding off and those on the phone or Web session will likely be doing other things and not paying attention. Engagement is not only vital to keep interest, but to help with learning.

When you plan to present a topic, try to find frequent opportunities to pause and engage the members on the points just made. I realize that sometimes you just need to present the material without interruption, so keep those presentations brief and then open up for discussion and follow up afterwards.

When many of your attendees are dialing in remotely, it can be hard to engage others verbally. Many will not even try to speak up, and talking over each other is a problem. Using online tools, you can engage your attendees with polls and other online collaboration tactics to gather input and keep them actively involved without having to unmute.

Until you know if your audience will actively participate, have a few *"plants"* – people you have prearranged to engage with to help encourage others to get involved.

Post Archives

One school of thought is you must be present to obtain the information. If every presentation is posted online, what is the incentive to show up for the meetings? If you are asking yourself that question, ask yourself this one as well – what is more important, that someone show up for a live meeting or that someone consumes the information? If it were that cut and dry, one or the other, I hope you would choose consumption of the information.

Video of the meeting presentation is one option. Another option is to do a voiceover on your presentation slides. Posting these to your CoI resource site makes them available to anyone that did not attend. If you are concerned that this easy availability online might encourage people to not show up to the live meetings, then do not *advertise* the fact that you have them at first. Stress for, and monitor, live attendance and determine how to proceed. If attendance is not what it should be, promoting the archives is one way to help encourage consumption of the information.

Repetition is Key

Transforming mindsets is a constant work in progress. Just as you would do something over and over to learn how to do that thing better, concepts also must be repeated and explained continuously. Often these two go hand-in-hand.

In my second case study, I mentioned that our first bite was more frequent review of work in progress. The practice of doing that review each month was not hard to learn and do consistently. The *why* behind it, however, needed repetition. For a team accustomed to being judged and penalized at every turn, in their mind, the review was just another way for them to be judged. In our mind, it was about do, experience, learn, and adjust. To change the development team's mindset around that practice, we needed to continuously talk about the value we were incorporating and demonstrate it through practice.

Once you find common ground on a principle, then you can begin looking at how that is being achieved with current processes and practices, and where you can start introducing alternative methods. We began the introduction to an empirical approach with monthly reviews and the team saw how those reviews caught issues early, allowing us to make adjustments. This does not mean the team never reverted back to previous thinking. To the contrary, but having a basic understanding of empirical thinking, we then could fall back on the question of how does this support a better product?

Old habits are hard to break, which is why repetition is key to bringing the mindset back to center. "What problem are we trying to solve" is one of my most used questions. The intent is to get off of solutions and onto the problem first, the real problem. Despite seeing mindsets shift tremendously toward this, or any new concept, I find that reminders are necessary. If repetition is still necessary in mature teams, how much more so is it needed in teams in the earlier stages of transformation?

Put Frameworks and Tools in Their Place

Frameworks are great starting places to help teach new concepts and put them into practice. The caveat, and the point I have tried to make throughout the book, is that it is far too easy for teams to get stuck inside a framework and specific tools. Scrum is very popular and relatively easy to do. It no doubt will help your team improve how it works in some way. That said, I do not believe you can reach the Ri stage of Agile inside of pure Scrum. If you cannot reach Ri, you cannot achieve Timeless Agility.

Do not let this keep you from using Scrum. Use what works from Scrum, learn how non-Scrum practices can fit your team and situation better, and just continuously seek to live out Agile values, principles, and concepts in ways that make sense for each team respectively. Keep *filling the gaps*.

In the "divided loyalties" case study in which I implemented monthly reviews and then monthly planning, we were not doing Scrum, but we borrowed some Scrum practices and used Scrum terminology around what we were doing in order to make progress. It helped the team learn and transition. Later in that case study, we moved away from Sprints, and most things Scrum, and developed continuously from a prioritized backlog – more Kanban style. Yet that team does not follow any one framework.

I think it is more important to understand what frameworks offer and how to leverage what you need, when you need it, than to get caught up in trying to adopt or implement anything specific wholeheartedly. This is easier said than done because it requires someone in the Ri stage to lead the teams. Helping the team determine what it should do, and how, is what coaches do. My advice to you is do not get caught up into the "Certification Economy" or feel the need to use popular tools. Do what makes sense for your teams, as they need it. Stay aligned with Agile, and you will be fine.

Chapter 10:
Measuring Success

What you measure says a lot about what you value. In Chapter Six, I wrote about the "unintentional intentional distortion of Agile." I believe that early adopters compromised with traditional-minded leaders. The result is that *"Agile metrics"* were created to provide the comfortable traditional measurements that organizations desired. The challenge is that organizations moving to Agile tend to:

- ❖ Force old metrics on new ways of working

- ❖ Misuse new metrics to fit old ways of thinking

- ❖ Use the common Agile metrics out of context

As I noted in Chapter Four, key success measures from the respondents of the *12th Annual State of Agile Report* included velocity, planned vs. actual stories delivered, and estimation accuracy. These metrics are still based on being *"productive"* and *"on time."* – neither aligns with Agile. Bad data leads to bad decisions.

If you will recall from Chapter Five, the crowd is rarely right. In this chapter, I will challenge the *"common wisdom"* and provide you with the measures I think tell a more accurate story about how your teams and product are doing.

Context is Everything

Are you familiar with the image below: is it a rabbit or a duck? It highlights the fact that perspective is important – context is everything. Similar to metrics and measurements, how you look at that data determines the story it tells. It is not always as clear as you might expect.

Follow me through a real-life basketball data analysis example to demonstrate this point. Carmelo Anthony, a NBA basketball player, was the highest scoring player on his team one particular year. Based on this data alone, it may seem obvious that he should have played every minute of every game. However, the team actually had a higher winning percentage when Carmelo *did not* play. Based on this last piece of data, it would be reasonable to wonder why the team did not trade him – the team won more without him in the game. How can two pieces of data lead to such opposite perspectives?

As it turned out, Carmelo was the highest scoring player because he took the most shots. His shooting percentage, however, was lower than other players on the team. This is why the team's winning percentage was less when he played. Overall, the team was taking lower-percentage shots. This additional data seems to further support the notion that the team should have removed Carmelo.

Digging deeper into the context of Carmelo's situation, we learn that the reason his shooting percentage was lower than his teammates was because he was often double- and triple-teamed. This means that two or three defenders guarded him when he had the ball. They did this because he was actually a very good shooter. When he was open, or only covered by one man, his shooting percentage was higher than his teammates. When double- and triple-teamed, his percentage was much lower. The problem was that Carmelo was still taking the highly contested shots.

What have you seen thus far regarding the context of the data? The initial surface data suggested that Carmelo should have played all the time because he was the highest scoring player. Additional data then led to the possibility that perhaps he should not play at all. Diving deeper, additional contexts around the data helped to conclude that Carmelo was valuable to the team, but he needed to make some changes. The answer was for Carmelo to take the shot when he was open, or only guarded by one defender, but pass the ball when double- or triple-teamed. When he did that, the team's winning percentage went up beyond what it was when he did not play.

Carmelo's individual statistics went down – he scored fewer points per game – but the team won more games. If we measured Carmelo by his individual numbers, his *"contribution"* went down, but we know that is not reflective of reality. Putting everything into context, we know that his contribution spoke far more than numbers and charts. We know that no one single indicator tells the whole story – that context is everything. We also know that tracking the wrong things leads to the wrong conclusions.

The same holds true for your product teams. When you turn your focus away from outputs and onto outcomes, your perspective changes. What you measure, and why you measure it, changes. You stop letting single graphs and data points tell you if you are successful. You look at everything with context.

What NOT to Measure

What I cover in this section, as what NOT to measure, is going to be just about every common *"Agile metric"* taught today. I want to start here because these are the metrics you are likely familiar with. Organizations track these metrics because it *seems* like the right thing to do – the Streetlight Effect. Measuring the wrong things in the wrong way not only tells the wrong story as-is, but it often leads to teams *"gaming"* the numbers to look better – the Hawthorne Effect. Ineffective measures become even more ineffective, and useless.

In this section, I will assess each measure just enough to demonstrate:

- ❖ What many people **think** the metric tells them
- ❖ What the metric **actually** tells them
- ❖ What the metric **does not** tell them

Outputs (Productivity)

Productivity has two primary meanings. It can be about *how much* of something is delivered (outputs). For example, the productivity of the team increased as they got faster at doing the work. Productivity can also be about the *effectiveness* of something delivered (outcomes). For example, the team's meetings are more productive now that they include the right people in the conversations.

Measuring a team's output production seems to be a good way to know if the team is working as efficiently as possible. Doing more seems like the right thing to pursue. These types of metrics might show a team getting better at delivering more output. However, the increase may simply be a result of padded estimates to meet performance targets. What it does not show is value delivered. An Agile mindset avoids measuring success by the team's outputs. Becoming more efficient is surely a goal, but success is measured by how frequently the most valuable software is delivered. This is not the same thing as getting more done in less time.

Traditional project management focuses on completing all the pre-planned work by the pre-planned dates. When scope is fixed and thorough analysis provides detailed estimates, the desire is to measure how well the team is doing against those projections. After all, teams have committed dates to keep, so increasing productivity promises more in less time. Despite the fact that few teams can accurately estimate the effort of knowledge work (e.g. software development) up front, this desire carries over into Agile practices. The resulting metrics include *velocity* and *burn down*.

Team Velocity

Think it tells how productive the team was/is.
Actually tells how many story points were delivered.
Does not tell how effective the team was/is.

Velocity is how much a team outputs over its iteration cadence, or Sprint if the team follows Scrum. It is the measure of how much was *done*, in terms of the original estimated value placed on the finished work. Teams may estimate in hours, but often they will estimate user stories in *story points*. The estimate provided for each story before development begins is what is captured as finished velocity when delivered. The actual effort is often different from the estimate, but the theory is that it all averages out over time.

Story points are an arbitrary unit of relative measure unique to each team. Some teams use the Fibonacci scale, which follows 1, 2, 3, 5, 8, 13, 21, etc., or some variation of it. It allows the team to rank stories based on relative size to each other without having to put too much effort into actual hours estimates. T-shirt size is another common relative estimation tactic, although t-shirt size tends to equate with a number for velocity calculation.

If the easiest story is given one story point by the team, then something twice as big will be given two story points. The team figures out what represents the easiest and hardest, and estimates stories relative to the other. Each story developed during a Sprint allows the team to claim its story points. The team's velocity is the total story points delivered during the iteration. A team good at estimating in this way can become consistent and fairly accurate at estimating which stories it thinks it can complete in a Sprint, or over several Sprints.

Understanding a team's velocity is not necessarily the problem. Using velocity as a management metric is the misapplication. It is nice to have a general idea regarding how much the team might be able to do in a given time period. However, using it as a measure of productivity keeps the team from experimenting, discovering, or focusing on the learning that occurs during development feedback. When a team focuses on these value-driven activities, they risk reducing *"productivity."* Punitive fear leads to protective behavior over doing what is best for the product.

Many **think** that velocity is an indication of how productive the team is. The goal becomes increased velocity iteration over iteration. Some will even compare one team's velocity to another, which has always been a faux pas. How each team relatively sizes stories is unique to each team. It is a metric unique to them. Even still, it is a very rough way to estimate the size of work. Yes, the team can become fairly accurate at working within a velocity range, but is that an indication of their *productivity*? Is the number of points Carmelo Anthony scores an indicator of his contribution?

What velocity **actually** tells you is how many story points the team completed – nothing more, nothing less. How you interpret that data, and its context, is everything. For starters, what does it mean to be productive? Is it more productive to get ten expected stories done, or to use discovery to take a different direction and get two stories done better than originally scoped? The first will give you more story points. The second will presumably give you a better product. Which is more *productive*?

Pressure to increase velocity pushes teams into the Hawthorne Effect – they will do what it takes to make the numbers look good. If you want more velocity, and the team is judged by velocity, then they may just pad their story point estimates. Is that helpful? Another undesired behavior is that the team may finish all committed work as planned as quickly as possible, despite what it may have learned along the way. What if the team discovers during development that there is a better way, or that the item should not be done at all? Is it ideal to complete it anyway, since it was a commitment? Does this behavior mean you should not track something that you think is important? No, but the question is, should you be tracking outputs rather than outcomes?

What velocity **does not** tell you is how much value your team is delivering. I suppose you could put the onus on the Product Owner and business for ensuring the development teams work on the most valuable work. This would free you up to treat the development team as a feature factory whose goal is to get progressively more work done in less time. If that is your focus, then I can see why velocity would be important. This approach is not Agile, however. Additionally, learning what not to deliver is also valuable, is it not? If your team discovered that something should not be done, or done the way the team initially thought, would learning that be valuable despite delivering fewer story points – less velocity?

Measuring velocity tends to tie into the desire to track outputs against a plan. This conflicts with, and hinders empirical development. I do believe understanding the team's velocity *can be* valuable to the development team. In the team's quest to get better, velocity is one data point to inform. I also believe velocity *can be* used to help make decisions about what to work on, and when, given anticipated effort. However, when management uses velocity for traditional output measures, the focus for success measurement is in the wrong place.

Individual Velocity

Think it tells how productive the developer was/is.
Actually tells how many story points were delivered.
Does not tell how effective the developer was/is.

Measuring individual velocity, or contribution, is similar in many ways to measuring team velocity. In both, management thinks it is an indication of productivity, but it fails to tell the whole story. I separate team from individual velocity because there are some specific false assumptions I think need special attention.

Many people *think* individual velocity is an indication of how productive the developer is. When an organization is focused on output productivity, it does so at both the team and individual level. The idea is that if each developer maximizes his or her capacity, then the team is maximized as a result. Velocity *actually* tells you how many story points the developer completed, but what it *does not* tell you is how valuable he or she really was/is to the team.

When you measure a developer's success by their personal output, when they are judged by that, you no longer have a *team*. Why would a developer turn away from their work to help another developer solve a problem that only the other developer will get velocity credit for? Go back to the Carmelo Anthony example. Why would he pass the ball and help teammates get open shots if he was solely judged by how many points he personally scored?

By measuring personal productivity, which seems like the right thing to do, you inadvertently create a group of individuals looking out only for themselves. This anti-pattern actually diminishes your effectiveness as a product team. Rather than teams rallying around tough problems to solve, they compete against each other. Rather than work on the most important work, they only pick up quick and easy work when given the choice – it gives them better velocity. It creates a culture of everyone for himself or herself.

Burn Down

Think it tells percent complete; schedule adherence.
Actually tells how much pre-planned work is done.
Does not tell if the right things are being delivered.

When teams move to Agile methods, such as short development iterations, they may move away from detailed project schedules to burn down charts. A burn down chart is a simple graphical depiction of how many committed stories, or story points, are complete and how many are remaining for the iteration. Burn down is typically tracked for a Sprint, but can also be tracked by release, which may consist of a few Sprints.

What many *think* a burn down provides is a view into percent complete, or schedule adherence. I suppose it does, based on the estimates given to each user story. They think it provides a schedule-tracking alternative. I suppose it does. I believe this is one of those compromises made to continue to give organizations a traditional tracking mechanism for Agile practices. I do not think it is a valuable metric.

What a burn down **actually** tells you is what you think it provides – how much is done and what is remaining. It is doing its job. With that data, you can estimate if your target deliverables will be completed when you planned. The concern is that it is often used to track "on-time delivery." Tracking to *on time* requirements can have negative consequences when not met – without regard for value delivered or learning. I cover *on time* in the next section as something not to measure.

What burn down **does not** tell you is the same as what any project schedule does not tell you. It does not indicate whether or not you are working on the right things at the right times. It does not account for employing an empirical approach. In fact, a focus on burn down, a focus on completing committed work, prevents teams from discovering better solutions during development. When an organization measures success by being on time with pre-planned work, the team's focus is on completing that work rather than exploring whether or not that is the right work to complete.

On Time

On time means that the planned work was completed within the planned timeline. When you track work via a schedule, that schedule only has meaning if there are specific tasks defined with specific dates. This is the only way to track whether or not something is *on time*. Burn down charts may be listed as an *"Agile metric,"* but can carry the same intentions as traditional project schedules – schedule adherence.

Schedule Adherence

Think it tells how successful the team is.
Actually tells how good or bad the team is at guessing.
Does not tell how effectively the team delivered value.

Schedule adherence and being on time has always been a major focus for project management. Full requirements are vetted and estimated. Large plans are built around each task. The team plans for dependencies and builds in contingencies. The project manager creates a baseline schedule and spends most of his or her time trying to keep the team on track with that schedule – to be *"on time."*

Many *think* schedule adherence is an indication of team efficiency and success. Projects are usually touted as successful when they finish on time.

Are all "on time" projects successful?
Are they unsuccessful if not "on time"?

Consider this example. The team is expected to deliver a specific set of requirements in six months. After two months, a requirement is found to be less effective than initially thought. There is discussion around not delivering it, or doing more discovery work to determine what would be a better solution. Management does not want to jeopardize scope and schedule, so they implement the feature as planned. They reason that this change is too big and thus it should be considered for phase two. One month later, someone proposes new requirements that seem timely based on user feedback. These seem like great ideas, but again, it would jeopardize scope and schedule to act on them. The change is too big and thus the request is deferred for phase two. After six months, all the planned scope is done, on time. Was this a successful project?

Consider another example. The team begins a Sprint with a goal to deliver stories one through five. After starting the first story, the highest priority, the team realizes that it is more complicated than estimated. The team has two options. They can focus solely on getting story one done, or they can defer it and get stories two through five done. Story one is just one story, so fewer story points will presumably be completed, but it is the highest priority item. Stories two through five will presumably have more story points, in addition to delivering more stories.

The team in this example has a value decision to make. Are stories two through five more valuable collectively than story one? Which option is better is a great conversation to have, but not the point I want to make here. My point here is this – neither option satisfies the criteria of *"on time."* So, is the team unsuccessful either way?

What schedule adherence ***actually*** tells you is how well, or how poorly, the team is at guessing. When you put a schedule together, or commit to five user stories for one Sprint, you are guessing. We can argue about the value of estimates and the quality and accuracy of estimates, but that is not the point. I have been very accurate in the past estimating work and schedules. I know it can be done. It is all still a guess. When your team finishes on time, it only means you did a good job guessing. When they do not finish on time, it only means you did not do a good job guessing.

What schedule adherence ***does not*** tell you is whether or not you delivered the right things. Similar to velocity, being on time ties into the desire to track outputs against a plan. This conflicts with, and hinders, an empirical approach.

Schedule adherence also **does not** tell you what you can expect from the team next time. To meet the schedule, the team may have had to work overtime. Quality may have been reduced to complete the work on time. Knowledge work is unpredictable. Many dates are arbitrary. Tracking to these dates does not inform you of anything except how well or how poorly you can guess, with the help of a little luck.

Projects

Think it helps control scope, budget, and schedule.
Actually creates unnecessary overhead.
Does not allow the team to work empirically.

The project management profession exists to ensure projects finish on scope, on budget, and on time. Many **think** success is tied to how well the project manager adheres to those three constraints. Is this a valid pursuit for software development?

Most project management jobs require the Project Management Professional (PMP)® certification. This certification is industry agnostic. Information technology project management, which includes software development, inherited many of the same practices as managing the construction of a skyscraper. If you have similar experiences as me, you know that fitting software development into traditional project management practices **actually** creates problems. For instance, how do you definitively plan around and manage knowledge work that inherently comes with unknowns?

The case management project I used as a case study in Chatpers Two and Eight is an example here. Contractually, it was considered a project. We were given a fixed budget and one year to build a case management system. Lucky for us, we were not given a detailed requirements specification.

Since the program needs were still fluid, we were able to proceed with iterative and incremental MVPs and use an empirical approach to do as much as possible within the time and money we had. We did not have fixed scope to deliver, so the definition of "on time" was blurred. We were instead looking to deliver as much value as possible for the time and money provided.

That is how software development should be. It is a product. Fund a team, which covers a time period, and evaluate the value delivered. If the team is producing value, and the stakeholders need more, continue to fund the team. An empirical approach is on ongoing practice of discovery. Products are used, feedback informs, and product teams should be continuously improving the product based on the needs of stakeholders. Projects simply do not fit this scenario. When fixed scope is not included, the concept of schedule adherence and *on time* no longer applies. It is no longer project management, but rather it is continuous product management.

There has always been a conflict with predictive scheduling in knowledge work. The *"need"* to track software development as projects is deeply rooted in traditional project management education. It seems right that you should predict and then track the work in order to control costs and timelines, but this approach **does not** support an empirical approach. I am not diminishing the need to understand what the organization gets for its money. There are ways to do that, beyond the scope of this book. Traditional project management, however, does not work well for software development. There are better ways to measure success and ensure you are getting the value for the money you want.

What You SHOULD Measure

In the previous section, I deemed everything you were taught about project management to be the wrong way to measure success from an Agile and software delivery perspective. So, what *should* you measure?

As a general rule, you should measure what helps you achieve your outcomes. Start with what you are trying to achieve and determine what you measure based on that. The paradox is that this is what many organizations are already doing. Outcomes and being on time are their objective, so they measure velocity and track schedules. The trick is to peel back the layers a bit and uncover what *really* matters.

In this section, I will assume being empirical matters. I will assume the Agile Manifesto matters. I will assume that doing the right things, more effectively, matters. I will assume Timeless Agility is the ultimate pursuit. With these objectives in mind, here is what I think you should measure:

- ❖ Agile transformation
- ❖ Value delivered
- ❖ Flow of value
- ❖ Risk

You deliver the right things, more effectively, and with less risk, when you follow an empirical approach. The flow of that value and how that informs the feedback loop for iteration is an important measure of your success. I will present ways to track how you are doing in these areas. I also believe that your team's transformation progress may be the single greatest measure of your success. With mindset transformation, and the resulting actions that flow from it, you automatically get the highest value delivered more frequently, continuous improvement, better quality, and motivated teams.

Agile Transformation

You should understand by now that Agile transformation from a Timeless Agility context is more about mindset than specific practices or frameworks. Transformation involves a mindset shift by each person within each team, including all levels of management. The whole reason to pursue Agile should be to work more empirically so that the right things are delivered more efficiently and with less risk. Each team will optimize differently, and the organization as a whole will need to learn new ways to support how all the teams collectively deliver on this objective. How well you do that is your primary measure of success. This measure alone can be a great indicator of how well you are delivering the right things.

Agile approaches presume reduced risk, higher and more frequent value delivered, better products, and higher quality. A team living out Agile well, by default, should bring about all those benefits. Measuring team health is a leading indicator of success that you can use to inform continuous improvement that ultimately leads to better product outcomes.

Team Health Survey

The team health survey is an activity to gauge how individuals within a team, group, or organization feel about specific areas of focus. These areas could be around your overall product management process, stakeholder engagement, teamwork, safety, continuous improvement, practices, performance, and more. This is a much broader view than a team retrospective and something you can track progress against over time. What you will look for in a team health survey is the trending, not so much the specific scores. The scores provide a snapshot of the current sentiment, but an upward trend is your goal. Downward and stagnate trends may indicate problems. This survey is just one piece of data to use with broader context to help you understand how the organization is doing and where additional improvement focus may be needed.

"When a measure becomes a target, it ceases to be a good measure." – Goodhart's Law

---

Given the nature of the questions, I recommend conducting the survey every one to three months. What you ask will depend upon what you want to track progress against. For example, here is a sample list of questions/statements you might consider for one of your product teams.

- ❖ Our team is empowered to deliver the most appropriate solutions for the organization.
- ❖ We effectively measure and confirm value delivered.
- ❖ I feel safe to openly discuss ideas or concerns.
- ❖ I feel safe to experiment and try new things.
- ❖ Our method of prioritization is effective and efficient.
- ❖ We appropriately engage each stakeholder group.
- ❖ I am provided with ample training opportunities.

The questions should cover topics such as empirical development, discovering the right things, learning, continuous improvement, safety, and practice. Using a 1-5 score, for strongly disagree to strongly agree, you can produce average scores for each question and grouping of questions. Trends over time are what I focus on.

The number of questions you ask will depend upon what you want to measure. The questions may also change over time. Some questions may be temporary to track something specific, while others remain due to their importance. As a general rule, you will want to stop capturing metrics when they have outlived their usefulness.

How you collect feedback to this survey will likely depend upon the survey tools you have available to you. Same for how you compile and present the data. It does not need to be elaborate or time-consuming. Here is an example display I have used from which to generate conversation.

	Nov-17	Feb-18	May-18	Trend
	4.08	4.16	4.17	⬆
Overall	4.15	4.23	4.00	⬇
Empowerment	3.90	4.00	3.80	⬇
Stakeholders		3.80	3.40	⬇
Measure of Success	3.90	4.00	4.20	⬆
Value-driven	3.90	4.50	4.60	⬆
Decision-making		3.80	4.00	⬆
Overall	4.16	4.26	4.52	⬆
Learning	4.30	4.50	4.60	⬆
Coaching	4.60	4.70	4.70	⇒
Safety	4.10	3.90	4.50	⬆
Feedback	3.90	3.50	4.40	⬆
Collaboration	3.90	4.00	4.40	⬆
Overall	3.85	4.11	3.80	⬇
Sustainable Pace	3.40	4.10	4.20	⬆
Value Delivered	3.70	3.70	3.70	⇒
Continuous Delivery	3.20	3.20	2.90	⬇
Continuous Improvement	4.20	4.56	4.40	⬇

As you can see, there are a couple of topic areas with no score from the November 2017 period. This is because the team only started focusing on that area with its February 2018 survey. Questions dropped from the previous period were dropped entirely from the list. It is shown as black and white here, but the measures use red, yellow, and green thresholds to gauge effectiveness.

There is always a narrative within the data. As a coach, I use this data along with comments provided, and simple observation, to gauge the context. Data and reports serve a purpose, but good old-fashioned observation and context bring it all together.

Observation Metrics

I am calling this *observation metrics*, but there really are not any recorded metrics involved. It is more contextual notes than metrics. Refer back to the Carmelo Anthony example again and consider how observation played a role in understanding what the data said. What the data could not convey is the context around the circumstances. Only observation could fill those gaps. The coaches observed the scenarios from which to conclude that Carmelo was indeed valuable in ways the data could not show. For example, since he was such a good shooter, defenders would leave other players open to cover him. This presented opportunities to pass to unguarded players that could take high-percentage shots. Observation explained why Carmelo's shooting percentage was lower, despite his high scoring numbers.

The value of observation to put context around the data cannot be overstated. This is why having a coach *"on the ground"* is so important – someone who can identify what is important, and interpret what is seen.

Measure Value Delivered

Traditional reporting tells you how much work was done in a given time period. Nothing in that reporting suggests that what was delivered was valuable, or the highest value that could have been delivered. You can assume that the team is always working on the most important work, but how do you really know that is true?

When you build your backlog and prioritize, you assume those are the most important, or highest-value stories, but they are really just assumptions. Perhaps you are able to place a monetary value on the proposed work. Perhaps you have calculated the *Cost of Delay*. Regardless of how much data you have to support the need for the requirement, it is an assumption until validated.

Cost of Delay is a derived value based on the total expected value of a thing with respect to time. In product work, Weighted Shortest Job First (WSJF) [20] is a technique that divides cost of delay by effort to help determine which work should be done first. This is a way to calculate the value of proposed work, but it still is only an assumption that needs to be validated.

Value delivered can only be measured post-deployment. There are a few options to provide insight into the value of what you are delivering, but again, these are post-deployment.

Net Promoter Score

A net promoter score is the percentage of people that would recommend your product. You capture this by asking, "Would you recommend this product...?" The second part of that question might be, "...to perform xyz functions," or "...to a friend or colleague." A simple yes or no question is more likely to receive a response and it serves as a satisfaction indicator. Users only recommend products they think are valuable.

User / Stakeholder Feedback

Capturing more detailed feedback from those who use or benefit from your product is a valuable satisfaction indicator. My experience is that the majority of people that leave feedback do so because they have a complaint. If you understand that, you can put the feedback in context.

Are there common themes to the complaints? Do you see those specific complaints reduce after deploying a change aimed at addressing that problem? If yes, that is an indicator that you are delivering value.

What percentage of those asked leave feedback? If you see a spike in the number or percentage of those leaving feedback, is that an indicator that something is wrong? Likewise, would fewer responses indicate you are delivering value since satisfied users tend not to submit feedback? I am making that assumption based on my own insight rather than industry data, and it will need to be something that you determine within your own context as well.

Feature Usage

How often are the features you deploy used? You had users requesting a feature. Your WSJF indicated that the feature should be built next, so you delivered it. Did you deliver value? Are users using the feature? Did they use it initially, but then usage dropped off? Why? Remember, all you could do before you built it was assume you knew what they wanted and that it was valuable. Validation comes post-production.

When you build new features, build them in ways to monitor usage. Features that are not used may not really be valuable. You will have to decide if maintaining that code is necessary. Perhaps this data will lead you to deploy more MVPs to test out assumptions first and empirically iterate from there. Perhaps you will remove unused features.

Measure the Flow of Value

Delivering value is one thing, but delivering it frequently is another. The flow of value from idea to production is called *Lead Time* and the flow from the start of development to production is called *Cycle Time*. Organizations should want to shorten both, and will need to improve their product development process, as well as deployment practices.

A Cumulative Flow Diagram (CFD) is used in Kanban to visualize the flow of work within a team. It is a snapshot of how many user stories or backlog items are in any given state at any given moment, with the exception that the "deployed" state is cumulative. In the CFD below, the first section is the size of the backlog. The last section, furthest right, is the cumulative deployed stories. The stages in between are the team's workflow stages, such as ready for development, what is in development, what is done, and what is pending deployment.

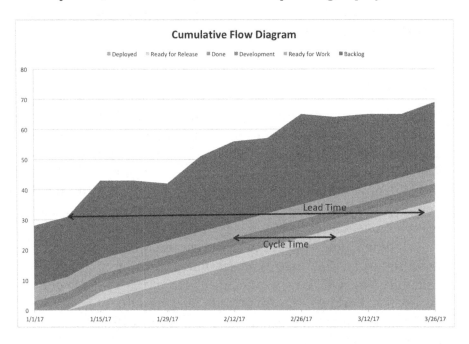

This is what continuous flow looks like, although few attain it. The smaller and more steady the swaths, the better, as it indicates a steady and continuous flow of work through each stage. Limiting how much work can be in each stage helps the team keep each swath small. The team's goal is to optimize its flow in order to focus on getting started work completed as quickly as possible. *Cycle Time* represents the time it takes for started work to reach production.

Lead Time is the *average* time it takes ideas to reach production. What the team works on is dependent upon its priority, or value, so ideas can enter your backlog and not be worked. In this example, the team has a large backlog. This could mean two things. Either the team is adding items to the backlog that are not valuable or there is more genuine demand than development capacity to deliver it.

There are two schools of thought here. One thought is that the backlog should remain small so that only ideas the team can work on relatively soon are present. Only high priority ideas would be added with this thinking – noting that if something is otherwise important, it will resurface later. This is still no guarantee that ideas inserted into the backlog will be done as they can just as easily be removed. I feel this approach artificially keeps *Lead Time* down.

The other thought is that anything the team *would do,* if it had the capacity, is added to the backlog. With this thinking, the size of the backlog is an indicator of demand. This means many backlog items will never get done since it should be prioritized by priority and value. New, more important stories will always rise above lesser-valued stories, regardless of age. You will have to decide if seeing that demand is valuable to your organization.

Both schools of thought align with the premise that *Lead Time* is not perfect since it does not convey a time period reflective of each backlog item. *Lead Time* is an average, where some items are worked quickly while others never make it to development. To provide more insight, you can track the age of individual backlog items. *Lead Time* may be six months but the oldest items may be two years old. Older items can become obsolete. Reviewing a large backlog is time-consuming and often not done. If you think a large backlog will help you demonstrate demand and get more development capacity, then you may want to take that route. Otherwise, keeping it smaller may work better for you.

The next CFD example portrays a team with great continuous flow up to the point of deployment. In other words, they do not deliver frequently, but rather do batch deployments about every two months. The bottleneck is clearly shown in the post-development stages. Organizations whose development teams move toward Agile practices, but their integration and operations teams do not, will exhibit this type of CFD. Implementing DevOps tools and processes will help.

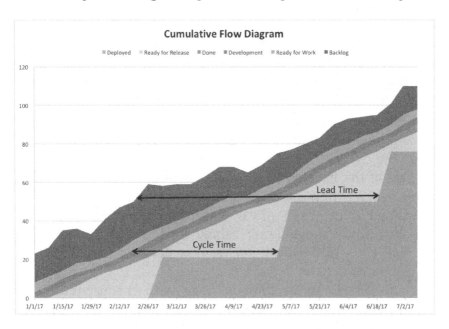

Measure Risk

Agile practices help to reduce risk naturally by working empirically and in short iterations, but they do not remove the need to track and manage risks. Risk can keep value from being delivered and/or from being delivered frequently. If something is going to fail, you will be better off facing those issues as early as possible. For example, you want to build on a new platform, but are concerned that it might have interoperability issues with integrated legacy systems. You do not want to learn this after all the other work is done. Moving risk forward is an approach for identifying the highest risks and working your way through them as early as possible. Sometimes approvals, especially from security and architecture governance teams, can bring everything you want to do to a halt. Identifying that risk early allows you to engage and address those concerns sooner rather than later.

Capturing your risks is just as important working in Agile ways as it was traditionally. The difference is that you will now work through the highest risk items first. Your estimated risk impact in relation to its probability of occurrence provides a risk score. Using these scores, you can rank your risks, and easily identify the ones to tackle first.

You can also track cumulative risk scores and average risk scores. This is another way to assess your overall risk exposure. Whenever there is a spike in risks, presumably due to adding new risks, you will want to see a steady and sharp decline in the overall risk scores. This indicates risk burn. Sharp increases in risk scores can also be the result of risks turning into issues. Similarly, you will want to resolve those issues and show steady risk burn down.

Carrying high risk, or worse, showing increasing risk, is an indicator that your value delivery is in jeopardy. Risk management is a topic beyond this book. However you do it, look to address and resolve the highest risk items first – keep your overall risk exposure low.

Conclusion

Agile values, principles, and other supporting concepts are without question timeless foundations for developing software products. An empirical approach of *do, experience, learn, and adjust* allows you to validate what you delivered, and learn from your miscalculations. After all, despite having great information about what you should work on next, it is still always just an assumption until it is validated. Working in short cycles to deliver something that can be experienced more frequently is the right objective. The ability to pivot to the next right thing based on learning is the heart of Agile. How teams learn to achieve this is through a variety of practices that improve collaboration, produce better code, and create a culture of continuous improvement. When would any of these things *not* be preferred? Therefore, Agile is not dead or something to run from. Rather, Agile is something to fight for and learn to live out correctly.

The struggle is real. The "Certification Economy" teaches frameworks and practices that are used to standardize how work is done. Management sends their development teams to training, but receive little to none themselves. The result is that traditional command and control thinking presses its thumb upon the teams trying to be more Agile. This leads to teams not liking Agile because they see it as just another way to do what did not work before – perhaps worse. In the end, their *"implementation"* of Agile is not really Agile, and the results reflect that.

Organizations think they want Agile but actively resist being completely Agile. They incorrectly hear something about getting more for less, or increased productivity, and glom onto that misinterpretation. To get some semblance of Agile *"in the door,"* early Agile proponents made compromises, which have proliferated industry and distorted the general understanding, and application, of Agile. What many organizations do, and measure, is more closely aligned with how they used to work than with the true meaning and intent of Agile. How success is measured is a clear indication of that thinking.

"Agile transformation" is another misused term due to its misinterpretation and application. Many organizations focus on scaling prescribed and standardized frameworks and practices. This tactic defies the Agile principle that suggests individual teams should be able to learn and adjust how they work. Standardized practices also come with standardized metrics that focus on outputs and productivity. Agile transformation becomes just another way to implement command and control within the organization. The term "Agile" is used, and so-called Agile practices are employed, but the intent behind it all remains traditional command and control with a push for more productivity. I wrote this book to help you understand where many have gone wrong with their view and understanding of Agile, and how to begin correcting course, if that describes your situation.

Hopefully you have assessed your organization, your teams, and yourself with regards to your understanding of the true meaning and intent of Agile values, principles, and concepts. At this point, you agree that an empirical approach is the center of everything you do in product management. Discovering the right things to do, at the right times, and learning how to deliver them more frequently is the overarching objective for your organization. You recognize that the Agile Manifesto is foundational and worthy to build upon. Exactly what you do and how you do it is no longer dogmatic.

What you do from here is take your first step. It is a journey – one that never really ends. I provided some starter information within this book, and the Resources section below will point you to additional sources of assistance. Where we used to have to convince our organizations to try Agile, today we have to correct the distortion, misunderstanding, and misapplication of Agile. This is not an easy job, but it is a worthy pursuit. Organizations that truly embrace and live out Agile, as intended, produce better products, have happier users and stakeholders, and possess a sought-after culture.

Thank you for taking the time to read this book and consider the perspectives of Timeless Agility. My hope is that it was well worth your time and that it helps you incite genuine Agile transformation where you are. Feel free to reach out to me (see resources) to let me know how your journey is coming along, or if you need any help.

Section 3: Resources

"Continuous learning is the minimum requirement for success in any field."
-Brian Tracy

Recommendations

Become a Member of Timeless Agility

Membership gives you exclusive access to Timeless Agility perspectives and insights. You are never alone in this journey when you are a Timeless Agility member.
Visit: https://timelessagility.com

Share Your Thoughts on Social Media

Use #PursuingTimelessAgility on your favorite social media platform to share your thoughts and comments with other readers of this book.

Write a Review on Amazon.com

If you like the book, please submit a review of the book at amazon.com. If you do not like the book, it is fair to write a review, but it will be most helpful if you submit your concerns to bookfeedback@timelessagility.com.

The Agile Manifesto

Internalize the Agile Manifesto values and principles:
http://agilemanifesto.org

About the Author

Jimmie Butler is a coach and consultant who specializes in helping teams and individuals be more effective and efficient. He challenges traditional thinking to help others see things in new ways. Mindset Transcends Methodology™ is a central belief. He guides and empowers others to find their way to meaningful transformation by establishing timeless foundational mindsets aligned with appropriate practices.

Jimmie has worked twenty-seven years across a variety of industries including federal government, healthcare, mortgage banking, non-profit / association, investment banking, manufacturing, and consulting for small businesses.

The vast majority of his experience is in helping software product teams discover and deliver the right things. He has gotten his hands dirty in the code from time to time, but has typically served as a project manager or a team lead on technical or development teams. He has extensive experience bridging the gap between technical teams and management with an eye on operational excellence.

References

[1] "Manifesto for Agile Software Development." Manifesto for Agile Software Development. http://agilemanifesto.org.

[2] Jeffries, Ron. "New Framework? XP Revised? No…" RonJeffries.com. September 17, 2018. https://ronjeffries.com/articles/018-01ff/new-framework-xp/.

[3] Jeffries, Ron. "The Manifesto is ancient history. Agile is alive and changing." RonJeffries.com. August 6, 2015. https://ronjeffries.com/articles/015-aug/manifesto/.

[4] Jeffries, Ron. "Developers Should Abandon Agile." RonJeffries.com. May 10, 2018. https://ronjeffries.com/articles/018-01ff/abandon-1/.

[5] Fowler, Martin. "The State of Agile Software in 2018: transcription of my keynote at Agile Australia." MartinFowler.com. August 25, 2018. https://martinfowler.com/articles/agile-aus-2018.html/.

[6] "Guiding Principles." Modern Agile. http://modernagile.org/.

[7] Schwaber, Ken, and Jeff Sutherland. *The Scrum Guide™*, 6. PDF. November 2017. https://www.scrumguides.org/docs/scrumguide/v2017/2017 -Scrum-Guide-US.pdf/.

[8] VersionOne. "Challenges Experienced Adopting & Scaling Agile." *12th Annual State of Agile Report, 12*. April 9, 2018, https://explore.versionone.com/state-of-agile/versionone- 12th-annual-state-of-agile-report/.

[9] Jeffries, Ron. "Scrum is not an Agile Software Development Framework." RonJeffries.com. July 19, 2018. https://ronjeffries.com/articles/018-01ff/scrum-not-asd-1/.

[10] "Scaled Agile Framework – SAFe for Lean Enterprises." Scaled Agile. https://www.scaledagileframework.com/

[11] "Planning Poker." Mountain Goat Software. https://www.mountaingoatsoftware.com/agile/planning- poker/.

[12] Schwaber, Ken, and Jeff Sutherland. *The Scrum Guide™*. PDF. November 2017. https://www.scrumguides.org/docs/scrumguide/v2017/2017 -Scrum-Guide-US.pdf/.

[13] VersionOne. "Percentage of Teams Using Agile." *12th Annual State of Agile Report, 6*. April 9, 2018, https://explore.versionone.com/state-of-agile/versionone- 12th-annual-state-of-agile-report/.

[14] VersionOne. "Percentage of Teams Using Agile." *11th Annual State of Agile Report, 7*. April 6, 2017, https://explore.versionone.com/state-of-agile/versionone-11th-annual-state-of-agile-report-2/.

[15] VersionOne. "Challenges Experienced Adopting & Scaling Agile." *12th Annual State of Agile Report, 12*. April 9, 2018. https://explore.versionone.com/state-of-agile/versionone-12th-annual-state-of-agile-report/.

[16] Wood, Urko. "Is the 'Street Light' Effect Keeping You From Success?" *The Business Journals*. January 15, 2016. https://www.bizjournals.com/bizjournals/how-to/growth-strategies/2016/01/is-the-streetlight-effect-keeping-you-from-success.html/.

[17] Cherry, Kendra. "The Hawthorne Effect and Behavior Studies." Verywell Mind, Dotdash Publishing. November 11, 2018. https://www.verywellmind.com/what-is-the-hawthorne-effect-2795234/.

[18] Hunt, Andy. @PragmaticAndy Twitter Feed. Twitter. 2/12/19.

[19] "Tuckman's Stages of Group Development." Wikipedia. https://en.wikipedia.org/wiki/Tuckman%27s_stages_of_group_development/.

[20] Reinertsen, Donald G. *The Principles of Product Development Flow: Second Generation Lean Product Development, 193*. Redondo Beach: Celeritas Publishing, 2009.

Made in the USA
Middletown, DE
23 June 2019